K
S

Marwan M. Obeidat ·
American Literature and Orientalism

ISLAMKUNDLICHE UNTERSUCHUNGEN · BAND 219

begründet

von

Klaus Schwarz

herausgegeben

von

Gerd Winkelhane

KLAUS SCHWARZ VERLAG · BERLIN

ISLAMKUNDLICHE UNTERSUCHUNGEN · BAND 219

Marwan M. Obeidat

American Literature and Orientalism

KLAUS SCHWARZ VERLAG · BERLIN · 1998

Die Deutsche Bibliothek – CIP-Einheitsaufnahme

Obeidat, Marwan M.:
American literature and orientalism / Marwan M. Obeidat –
Berlin : Schwarz, 1998
    (Islamkundliche Untersuchungen ; Bd. 219)
    ISBN 3-87997-271-0

© Gerd Winkelhane, Berlin 1998.
Klaus Schwarz Verlag GmbH, Postfach 41 02 40, D-12112 Berlin
ISBN 3-87997-271-0
Druck: Offsetdruckerei Gerhard Weinert GmbH, D-12099 Berlin

ISSN 0939-1940
ISBN 3-87997-271-0

AMERICAN LITERATURE
AND ORIENTALISM

Marwan M. Obeidat is Associate Professor of American literature presently at the United Arab Emirates University. He received his Ph.D. in American literature from Indiana University, Bloomington. He is member of the Organization of American Historians, and he also serves as International Co-Editor of both *The Journal of American History* as well as *Connections: American History and Culture in an International Perspective* (USA).

Preface

In the nineteenth century, there was a massive influx of Near Eastern material into American literature. Lacking immediate contact with the region, American authors had little accurate knowledge of it, and the result is that the factual content of writings dealing with the Muslim Orient is weak or distorted. Islamic material was not accompanied by accurate representations of Muslim manners, and the image of the Muslims that was formed by many authors of the time is often sternly unflattering, even if weakly grounded in knowledge. The religion and the Prophet similarly remain shrouded in legend, vagueness, and prejudice.

Serious in-depth scholarly investigation has not yet been made on the subject of the influence of the Muslim East in nineteenth-century American literature. There are only very few studies, each covering but a meager portion of the subject. Such studies include Frederic I. Carpenter's *Emerson and Asia* (1930), Arthur Christy's *The Orient in American Transcendentalism* (1932), Dorothee M. Finkelstein's *Melville's Orienda* (1961), David H. Finnie's *Pioneers East* (1967), and Franklin Walker's *Irreverent Pilgrims: Melville, Browne and Mark Twain in the Holy Land* (1974). None of the aforementioned works regards the Muslim Orient as an independent phenomenon that could be looked at from a broader perspective, a perspective that could be related to the larger concerns of American literature. Since virtually no comprehensive critical research has been undertaken to explore the area, my treatment is both investigatory and

3

exploratory. Its main focus is the literary record of an array of authors who dealt with the subject, and one of my principal aims is to bring together material which, because of its specialized Orientalism, has not entered the mainstream of scholarship and ascertain the image of the Muslim Orient to see what Islam and the Muslims meant to Americans.

My introductory chapter looks at the historical and cultural interrelations between the Christian West and the Muslim East and it considers the perceptions and uses of the Near Orient in the English and European literary tradition, including such background as *Poem of the Cid* (1140) and Dante's *The Divine Comedy* (1314). More immediately, drawing in part on such careful investigations as Byron Smith's *Islam in English Literature* (1939), I survey English romantic Orientalism as exemplified in Robert Southey's *Thalaba* (1801), Lord Byron's *Childe Harold's Pilgrimage* (1809-1818) and *The Giaour* (1813), and Thomas Moore's *Lalla Rookh* (1817). This chapter concludes with a summary view of the impact of the Barbary conflicts on early American nationalism and culture which furnished the theme of Royall Tyler's *The Algerine Captive* (1797) and other contemporary literature.

Against this literary and cultural background, the book proceeds to a chapter examining Washington Irving's romantic conceptions of the mystery and attractiveness of Muslim Spain. Here I consider *The Conquest of Granada* (1829) and *The Alhambra* (1832). Irving's immensely popular introduction of such romantic material was followed by a biographical and historical treatment of *Mahomet and His Successors* (1849-50), which in turn led to further popular literature such as *Mohammed, the Arabian Prophet* (1850) by George H. Miles.

The third chapter considers Emerson, whose interest in the Muslim Orient is at variance with the romance of Irving's Orientalism. The involvement of Emerson in Oriental thought is essentially part of the beginnings of comparative religion as a field for study, but it goes beyond that. In Emerson's case there is a particular interest in, and admiration for, the Sufi poets. Contemporary with Emerson, Whittier, not concerned primarily with Islam and the Muslims or their philosophy and literature, illustrates yet a different emphasis in connection with the antislavery movement, and he complements the image of the period.

In the fourth chapter, I examine works on the region as described by those numerous travelers who visited it. Among the works I consider are Nathaniel P. Willis' *Pencillings by the Way* (1836), John L. Stephens' *Incidents of Travel in Egypt, Arabia Petraea, and the Holy Land* (1837) and *Incidents of Travel in Greece, Turkey, Russia and Poland* (1838), George W. Curtis' *Nile Notes of a Howadji* (1851) and *The Howadji in Syria* (1852), John Ross Browne's *Yusef; or,* the *Journey of the Frangi* (1853), Bayard Taylor's *A Journey to Central Africa* (1854) and *The Lands of the Saracen* (1855), John W. De Forest's *Oriental Acquaintance; or, Letters from Syria* (1856) and *Irene, The Missionary* (1879). In varying degrees these travelers added no particular information of a specific, differentiating kind. But, though sometimes fanciful, they popularized the Muslim Orient. Later in the nineteenth century, Mark Twain in *The Innocents Abroad* (1869) and Melville in *Clarel* (1876) make major use of the Near Orient.

While Mark Twain's book is a classic of American humor, Herman Melville's poem is deeply serious and especially interesting in its philosophical use of the setting he observed on a trip to Palestine (1857).

In the fifth and final chapter, I summarize this development and greater definition of interest in the Muslim Orient in nineteenth-century American literature. This chapter, however, suggests briefly how the nineteenth-century American development of an idea of the Muslim East has continuities and reiterations even into the recent past as reflected in such books as Kenneth Roberts' *Lydia Bailey* (1947), Laurie Devine's *The Nile* (1983), and Leon Uris' *The Haj* (1984).

Acknowledgments

The present work sets out to explore extensively nineteenth-century American literary perceptions and/or experiences of the Arab World to see what Islam and the Muslims meant to America and to American authors during that period of history. This book complements a series of articles that were published in the past few years; with these other works *American Literature and Orientalism* shares a common theme, namely, that American literary representations of the Muslim world (or the Middle East, as some prefer to say) distort both Islam and the Muslims.

The five chapters and the bibliography that make up the book have appeared in various academic referced journals in the United States and in Europe, as follows:

Chapter 1 appeared in *The International Journal of Islamic and Arabic Studies* (Indiana University, Bloomington, U.S.A., 32, 2 (1985): 47-67), as did Chapter 2 (4, 1 (1987): 27-44); Chapter 3 appeared in *The Muslim World*

(Hartford Seminary, Hartford, Connecticut, U.S.A., 68, 2 (1988): 132-145); Chapter 4 appeared in *Der Islam* (The Institute for Islamic and Oriental Studies, Hamburg University, Hamburg, Germany, 68, 1 (1991): 115-126); and Chapter 5 appeared in *American Studies International* (George Washington University, Washington, D.C., U.S.A., 26, 2 (1988): 25-36).

I am grateful to the editors and publishers of these articles for permission to reprint this material.

I would like to acknowledge, with utmost gratitude, the ever-helpful and encouraging Professor Mohammad H. Asfour of the Department of English Language and Literature, University of Jordan, my friend, teacher, and colleague, who has always assured me that this book would see the light of day sometime!

Also I gratefully acknowledge the valuable comments of colleagues and friends at various universities in the Arab World and abroad: their questions and discussions enhanced the manuscript considerably. Any mistakes that remain are my responsibility alone.

Wallace E. Williams, James H. Justus, and Terrence Martin of Indiana University, Bloomington – subtle Americanists all – first interested me in American literature. This book owes much to the many kindnesses of a number of friends, colleagues, and students in Jordan as well as in the United Arab Emirates.

My principal debt is to Tagreed; her love, patience, and support made much of the work on this book managable, and to my children, who must have felt they had lost "dad" to a P.C. To Tagreed, then, Amr, Isra, Asem, and Ala'a Obeidat, whose presence has been a delight – in and of itself – this work is dedicated. Nor are my parents forgotten.

Contents

For between the Moors and Christians
Long has been the fight and sore.
                    Longfellow, *Translations*

There stood the infidel of modern breed,
Blest vegetation of infernal seed,
Alike no Deist, and no Christian, he;
But from all principle, all virtue, free.
To him all things the same, as good or evil;
Jehovah, Jove, the Lama, or the Devil;
Mohammed's braying, or Isaiah's lays;
The Indian's Powaws, or the Christian's Praise.
                    Timothy Dwight,
                    The Triumph of Infidelity

The Turks have a second-rate religion; they
are fatalists, and that keeps them down.
                    Henry James,
                    The Bostonians

Chapter One:

Introduction: The Cultural and Historical Background

Up to 1699, the year which marked the end of the centuries-long Ottoman threat to Europe, when the Treaty of Karlowitz between the Ottoman Empire and Austria, Poland, and Venice was signed, it was through hostility and suspicion the Christian West tended to view the Muslim East.[1] Outright hostility results in prejudice, and prejudice in dislike. It is not surprising, therefore, that the Christian West eleborated its cultural and intellectual polemic against Islam. This began in popular forms, but after the initial success of the West in Spain and the beginning of the Crusades, Christian men of letters produced unflattering representations that amount to what can be called a "distorted image"[2] not only of Islam as a religion, but also of the Muslims. As well be clear in this chapter, among their emphases or assertions were that Islam was practically a religion of violence, that Muhammad was the author of a false religion based on deceit, and that the Muslims were more or less infidels identified with the devil.[3]

This distorted image dominated most Western thinking until the later nineteenth century and even still has not completely lost its influence. Nevertheless, to some degree, a more tolerant, more sympathetic image of Islam has been attained through the work of genuine scholars acquiring more accurate information, and partly through the growing understanding of Islam as a religion.[4]

Meredith Jones remarks, "The [Western] conception of Mahomet and his teachings came more from literary sources than from actual observations of the Moslem people.... Usually writers drew on obscure or second-hand sources, and the result is a combination of a little fact and much imagination of a very biased character."[5] These sources were, to a large degree, provided by those who escaped the advancing Muslim armies on several fronts, and whose religious zeal prevented them from presenting an accurate picture of Islam. As Muslim power in Spain diminished, an even more serious threat, the Ottoman Turks, was menacing Europe from the East. The Muslim Turks gained a strong foothold on the frontiers of Christendom, ravaging or threatening half of Europe, and further expansion was always possible. The Crusades had not accomplished much in terms of either military or religious achievement. But the Christians became aware that there was a strong formidable enemy, who was culturally far superior to them and whose military might was redoubtable beyond the imagination.

For a considerable time Christendom had little knowledge of Islam. Mahound, a deformation of the Prophet's name, was consistently identified with the devil. While the Crusades created greater demand for in-depth knowledge of the enemy, what was known of Islam was second-or-third-hand information at best, and usually a caricature. The Muslims, cast in the role of the enemy, must, of course, be fierce and irrational. In brief it was an "age of ignorance," to use R.W. Southern's words,[6] during which all that was known about Islam was inspired by the view that the rule of the Muslims was a preparation for the final appearance of Antichrist. Actually by the early nineteenth century Western views of Islam had long been distorted. These views practically went all the way back to the Middle Ages, when the Prophet and the religion appeared in polemic writings, and the Muslims, almost universally known as the Saracens,[7] figured in contemporary popular literature.

Dorothee Metlitzki Finkelstein rightly observes that the first subtle impact of an idea of the Muslim Orient on the Latin West "was brought about by the most dramatic confrontation of East and West in the Middle Ages--the Crusades."[8] The Crusades (1095-1291) placed in sharper confrontation Western stances and Islam. The Crusading movement was motivated by religious propaganda to arouse the passions of the Christians to take the Cross against the Muslims. Such propaganda was, for example, used by Pope Urban II in 1095 for aid against "the infields," and earlier by Pope Gregory VII in 1075.[9] Later the propaganda against Islam took on a new form. Peter the Venerable, Abbot of Cluny, considered it necessary to counteract the present tendencies by refuting the beliefs of Islam and the portrayal of the character of the Prophet. Interest in the beliefs and doctrines of the Muslims had already been aroused. In his visit to Spain, about 1141, Peter the Venerable witnessed the civilization of the Saracens and determined to translate the Qur'an to see what it offered.[10] As could be expected in that age, the translation, made by three Christian scholars, together with an Arab, was inaccurate and full of errors. But it was the first major attempt in the West until almost the opening of the eighteenth century, when George Sale's version of the Qur'an appeared in London in 1734.[11] Peter the Venerable's work was frequently imitated, and polemical writings appeared in various forms; the aim of these polemics was, of course, not only to refute the Qur'an, but also to ridicule it. Peter's attempt, however, did much to perpetuate false beliefs about, and hostile attitudes towards, the Prophet and Islam that become common from the thirteenth century onward.

10

Though there are records here and there of earlier controversies, both oral and written, the first remarkable Christian polemicist to enter the field against Islam was John of Damascus (d. 749). His philosophical work on the *Sources of Knowledge* includes an important chapter, "Concerning Heresies," that deals with the Muslims.[12] John regarded the Prophet, like many of his medieval successors, as a Christian heretic, a false prophet, an utterly ignorant, shameless liar. More extensive, typical of much later controversy, is John's "Dialogue between a Christian and a Saracen."[13] The dialogue is concerned mainly with the theological question as to whether the Word of God is created or uncreated. The Saracen, when he hears the question, will flee because he has no answer. In the second half of the ninth century a harsher kind of polemic by Nicetas of Byzantium appeared. Nicetas tried his hand at a refutation, as James Addison points out, of "the foolish and infamous book of the Arab Mohammed."[14] Nicetas' work is essentially directed towards showing the fundamental truths of Christianity. Muhammad and the Qur'an are bitterly attacked, and the Muslims, according to Nicetas' beliefs, are so far astray in heresy!

The introduction of such polemic literature in the eighth and ninth centuries was followed by further literature in the period of the Crusades, which is a period characterized by persistent warfare. For two centuries Christendom, off and on, met the Muslim Orient as an enemy in the field. The religion was depicted as inferior, and the Prophet as a lustful, voluptuous, veritable devil.[15] It demanded an excessively high degree of objectivity to be reasonably fair to a hated foe. Towards the end of the thirteenth century William of Tripolis wrote *On the Condition of the Saracens*, in which, even if it shows opposition to Islamic beliefs and doctrines, he discusses certain points on which Islam and Christianity are virtually in agreement. And the contemporary Ricoldus de Monte Crucis, a scholar and a professor, wrote a popular treatise on *Confutatio Alcorani*. The work expresses hostility toward Islam and attacks the Qur'an and the sexual "immorality" of the Muslims. Other notable Medieval missionaries include as well Ramon Lull (1235-1315), who wrote extensively on the matter.[16]

The attitude of the Christian polemicists has, in varying degrees, remained the same until relatively recently: to attack Islam by means of discrediting it. "The points in which Islam and Christianity differ have not changed", suggests Norman Daniel in his masterly work on the subject, "so that Christians have always tended to make the same criticisms; and even when, in relatively modern times, some authors have self-consciously tried to emancipate themselves from Christian attitudes, they have not generally been as successful as they thought themselves."[17] The points on which Islam and Christianity are not in agreement are few, but crucial. Islam repudiates the divinity of Jesus; it even refuses to accept the Christian belief that he was crucified, thus denying the basic Christian doctrine of the Savior. Also, while it forced celibacy upon its clergy to follow the example of Christ, the church might be appalled at the Islamic law that any Muslim can marry four women at a time, with the Prophet having even more privileges in this respect. And again, though it did not advance by means of mere violence, Islam did teach that the cause of God was worth fighting for (Christianity, for two centuries, did resort to military crusading.) These points are only a meager portion of the polemic against Islam; the rest being a fanciful discourse directed towards receptive and unquestioning populace.

Norman Daniel also writes: "Whatever in Islam was most repellent to the Christian seemed to him also to be the most typical of it, and it was easy to set up standards against which all prophethood might be tested and Muhammad's be dismissed."[18] The polemicists tended to take certain events in the Prophet's life to cast doubt upon his credentials of prophethood. They alleged that he was not a prophet of God and related at length his many marriages, affirming his sensuality, and, simultaneously, contrasting it with the purity of Christ. They concluded that he was an impostor as a Prophet, since he showed no miracles. Muhammad was in addition presented as a Christian heretic. Often given deformed names,[19] he was said to be a member of ignoble trinity. It was also frequently related, in literary and biographical treatments of the Prophet, that he had trained a dove to eat grain from his ear, simulating the Holy Ghost, and, if not so, that he had trained a bull or a calf to come to his bidding, bearing the Qur'an bound to its horns.[20] Similarly, Islam is often described as the invention of a pagan god who presides over a larger body of other pagan gods; these include Feraon, Platon, Pilate, Jupin, Jupiter, Baratron, and many others. And the Muslims are often referred to as having an organized clergy, with a pope at its head, and with rituals conducted in Mahomeries (i.e., Mosques) in a way that is similar to the Christian rituals. By and large, Islam is viewed as a corrupt form of Christianity. And much was made of the supposed idolatry of the Muslims. Widespread was the belief that they worshipped Muhammad as a god, and that they had other gods and idols.

It would be just to say, then, that the Christian polemicists presented a reductionist picture of Islam and its Prophet, one of a totally incoherent nature. To quote Meredith Jones again, the medieval "conception of Islam was based on ecclesiastical authorities, whose interest in it was to disfigure the beliefs and customs of the infidels."[21] The disfigured image of "the infidels" emerged so often in the popular literature of the Middle Ages that it soon became a stereotype, inaccurate, unflattering, and unsympathetic. And Jones summarizes the stereotype of the Muslims that figured in the *Chansons de Geste* thus:

12

[The Muslims] are evil people, they spend their lives in hating and mocking at Christ and in destroying His churches. They are the children of the author of all evil, the Devil; like their ancestors, they hated God and are constantly placing themselves under the protection of Satan.... They are frequently presented as physical monstrosities; many of them are giants, whole tribes have horns on their heads, others are black as devils. They rush into battle making weird noises comparable to the barking of dogs. They are intensely emotional and excitable people, readily giving way to tears of joy and anger, always going from one emotional extreme to another. Socially, they are the embodiment of all foul practices, simply because they lack the one thing necessary in Christian eyes for perfection--belief in Christianity. Thus they use slaves, they eat their prisoners, they buy and sell their womenfolk; and they practice polygamy, which later, of course, they did in reality. The poets invent for them a host of insulting epithets and periphrases--which are little more than conventional epic phrases--to emphasize the unbelief which is the secret of all their wickedness.[22]

Such an image, distorted as it is, hardly demands any commentary on my part.

In Dante's *Inferno* the Prophet and Ali, the Prophet's cousin, are consigned to the ninth bolgia of the eighth circle of Hell among the schismatics.

While my gaze was on him occupied,
He looked at me, and with his hands laid bare
His breast. "Behold how I am rent," he cried.
"Yea, mark how is Mohammad mangled. There
In front of me doth Ali weeping go,
Ripped through the face even from chin to hair.
And all the rest thou seest with us below
Were sowers of schism and dissension, too,
During their lives, and hence are cloven so."[23]

J.S.P. Tatlock perceptively observed that such a treatment "is not only the most hideous mutilation of all in this valley; it is hardly equalled anywhere in the *Inferno* for repulsiveness, certainly not for ignoble bodily exposure and grotesqueness of description."[24] The harsh punishment of the Prophet stems from

13

the Christian view that Muhammad is a sower of discord and scandal. Other prominent Muslims whom Dante includes in the first circle of Hell, among the virtuous pagans, include Avicenna, Averroes, and Saladin (IV). The first two are philosophers, and the third is the champion of the Muslim cause against the Crusaders. The reasons why Dante places Saladin where he is (not in the eighth circle of Hell) is obvious: while a pagan (i.e., unbaptized) Saladin was also noble and virtuous, and thus in the first circle, together with the other two renowned philosophers, he has a relatively easy punishment, being denied the light of God.

The distorted conception, however, had long prevailed in the earlier European literary tradition. These portraits of Muhammad, the characterizations of the Qur'an, and the images of Islam remain typical: the Prophet is generally displayed as an impostor, the Qur'an as his fabrication, and Islam as a Christian heresy. As early as 1100, in a French epic poem, *La Chanson de Roland*, we find swine and dogs eating "Mahumet." The swine story was popular then; it furnished the explanation of the Qur'anic prohibition of eating pork. Another version gives the swine a chance while the victim lay unconscious in an epileptic fit. Still another substitutes drunkenness for epilepsy, explaining the Qur'anic injunction against wine. In any case, *Roland* is, more or less, a crusading poem that transforms the Basques, who, in 778, attacked Charlemagne's army, into Saracens. That these Saracens are prototypes of the infidels whom the Crusaders fought in the Holy Land is revealed when a reference is made to one of the Saracen knights: "He took Jerusalem by treachery" (cxviii).[25] While there is no clear indication as to who these Saracens may be ethnically, they are characterized by hostility to Christendom and by their acceptance of a corrupt form of Christianity. Such views, biased and prejudiced as they are, have been exploited in the poem as a source for artistic enrichment. The poem also employs a set of analogies. If the Christians have a trinity, so do the Saracens. If the French army has twelve peers, the Saracens too have theirs (lxxviii). The set of analogies we have in the poem is given through a series of contrasts: heathendom vs. Christendom, evil vs. good, the army of Christ vs. the army of Muhammad. The poem then moves to another subject: conversion. A Saracen knight is in fact depicted as having the qualifications of an admirable Christian knight: "Christian, he would excel in Chivalry" (lxxii). By the end of the poem "over a hundred thousand [infidels] are baptized/ True Christians, except for the queen." The reason why the Saracen queen is excluded is that Charlemagne wants her "through love to take the faith" (cclxvi). Following conversion the queen, Bramimonde, assumes a new name, Juliane. Concluding the poem by having the Saracens converted suggests not only religious, but a cultural triumph as well.

14

Similar, though different in form, is the *Spanish Poem of the Cid* (1140). The poem has the same issue *The Song of Roland* has; the Christian vs. the Muslim. When we first meet Yusuf, the king of Morocco, we see a man leading "an army of infidel hordes" (ii, 89).[26] But, unlike *Roland, The Cid* has contradictory implications. On the military level, the Christian Cid (a version of the Arabic Sayyid, i.e., "Master") more often fights the Moors, but at other times he appears to fight both Moors and Christians: "both Moors and Christians go in fear of me" (iii, 122). Yet the Cid has Moorish friends, such as the governor of Molina, Abengalbon. Cid's friendship for the Muslim Abengalbon is misplaced here, since he defies the Moors generally. But such a friendship may be looked at as incongruous, for not only is the Cid a redoubtable enemy of the Moors, but he is a Christian as well. Be this as it may, other characters in the poem, as in the case of the Cid's sons-in-law, the *infantes*, do, on the other hand, plot against both Moors and Christians. The Cid's sons-in-law "plotted an act of treachery" (iii, 126) in abandoning the Cid's daughters, and, once in Molina, in plotting Abengalbon's death to get hold of his wealth. Such literature is, of course, the immediate consequence of a cultural contact between the Christian Occident and the Muslim Orient.

John Lydgate's (1370?-1451?) "Off Machomet the false prophet and how he beying dronke was deuoured among swyn" is one of the earliest treatments of the Prophet in the English literary tradition. Lydgate incorporates a number of the contemporary legends and myths about the prophet. Here Muhammad is viewed as a magician of low birth who studied the Bible in Egypt. He claimed that he was "Messie" (1, 75), leading his followers astray. He was an epileptic who believed that "Gabriel / Was sent to hym from the heuenli mansioun / Be the Hooli Goost to his instruction: / For the angel shewed hym so sheene, / To stonde upright he myte nat susteene" (11. 87-91). The dove that picks grain from the prophet's ear and the bull that carries the Qur'an are also mentioned. And finally Muhammad

> Like a glotoun deied in dronknesse,
> Bi excesse of mykil drynkyng wyn,
> Fill in a podel, deuoured among swyn.
> (11. 152-4)[27]

Elizabethan literature, using or misusing Islamic material, utilizes two legends about Islam that had already accumulated in the European tradition.[28] Francis Bacon, for example, sees Muhammad as a miraclemonger. In "Of Boldness" Bacon tells us of the story of a miracle that did not come off. He writes:

15

Mahomet made the people believe that he would call a hill to him, and from the top of it offer up prayer for the observers of his law. The people assembled. Mahomet called the hill to come to him again and again; and when the hill stood still he was never a whit abashed, but said, "If the hill will not come to Mahomet, Mahomet will go to the hill."[29]

Even though the Qur'an unequivocally denies that the Prophet had any such gift, Bacon suggests that the legend existed, in a way, in the Islamic popular lore. At any rate, at the time the Ottoman Empire was at the gates of Europe, and Islam was seen more threateningly as the religion of the Ottoman Turks than that of the Saracens. To Western Europe, the Muslim Turks seemed a threat and they were viewed as fierce by nature. A humane Turk, should one meet one, would be an exception! As a result, the inhumanity of the Turks was emphasized above all else, and the stereotyped Turk--savage and bloodthirsty-- was firmly established in the literary tradition of the West.[30] Thus the word (Turk) suggested little more than cruelty and treachery in the eyes of the Christian West; it connoted absence of morality and religion and it represented, as Robert Schoebel suggests, the enemy of the Cross, the treacherous infidel, and the new barbarian.[31] Paul Coles observes, on the other hand, that "as one moved westwards into the hinterlands of European society, the Ottomans became increasingly the object of loathing and fear.... The Turks, it was argued, were beyond the pale not merely of Christianity, but of civilization itself."[32] This view was maintained and popularized during the sixteenth and later centuries. But whether it was known in the West that the Ottomans tolerated Christendom, and that, for humane reasons, they were looked upon by the peoples of the Balkan area as liberators from greedy land-owners, is not my point here. But it is my concern to show that the Renaissance image of the Turk was only a stereotype of European invention, as was the image of the Saracen in the preceding Medieval literary tradition.

The Turkish threat, i.e., the Islamic, was at its highest when Christopher Marlowe wrote his two-part play, *Tamburlaine* (Part I in 1587-8 and II in 1588; published in 1590). In Marlowe's "glorious hero," to use Byron Smith's words, "the theatre-goers saw not only the apotheosis of the will to power, but also a victor who had triumphed over a Turkish emperor, an augury perhaps of Christian conquests.[33] Marlowe was obviously working on public feelings; the hero, Tamburlaine (Taimur Lenk), not only humiliated the Turkish emperor, Bajazeth, but he also wanted to give relief to the conquered Christians in Constantinople, who had long been under siege. Thus Marlowe, as Smith rightly suggests, created a hero who could, the Christians would like to believe, take the Cross against the infidels and would also play the role of the instructor at the same time. So, ironically enough, the Muslim Tamburlaine is presented as a semi-pagan hero, well-read in classical tradition, utterly unkind to the Muslims, and, on the other hand, inexplicably responsive to the Christians and their heroic aspirations.

In Part I, Tamburlaine makes a promise that he "subdue the Turk."[34] And, in Part II, as soon as Babylon is threatened by the army of Tamburlaine, the citizens plead to their governor to

> Offer submission, hand up flags of truce,
> That Tamburlaine may pity our distress,
> And use us like a loving conqueror,
> Though this be held his last day's dreadful siege,
> Wherein he spareth neither man nor child,
> Yet are there Christians of Gerogia here,
> Whose state he never pitied and relieved
> Will get his pardon, if your grace would send.
> (II, V, i, 26-33)

The dominant anti-convention mode of the play suggests, among other things, an idea of re-ordering the world, awkward though it may be. Thus when liberating Tamburlaine is contrasted with the Muslim governor, who is exceptionally brutal against the Christians, the sympathy of the audience is likely to be won by Tamburlaine in spite of his cruelty. A point that should also be emphasized here is that all of Tamburlaine's victories are scored against Muslims, which would make it even more convenient for a Christian audience to identify with him, both emotionally and culturally.

Yet, in the Second Part of the play, Tamburlaine swears by Muhammad. If he had been a Muslim from the start, his zeal for the Christian cause is one that cannot be explained. But, on the basis of given evidence, it would be more adequate to say that there is little of Islam in him and in the rest of the Muslim characters of the play. Tamburlaine eventually renounces his religion.

> Now, Casane, where is the Turkish Alcoran,
> And all the heaps of superstitious books
> Found in the temples of that Mahomet
> Whom I have thought a god? They shall be burnt. [35]

It is more plausible, therefore, that Tamburlaine denounce Muhammad and burn the Qur'an. On either score, the harsh language used in the speech quoted above

17

would have probably won the sympathy of an audience that longed for the downfall of the world renowed enemy of Christendom, embodied at the time in the Ottoman Turks and their religion. And the play was popular because Tamburlaine not only defeated the Turks, but in his sad career (for it is a tragedy of one corrupted by power) also rejected Islam finally.

The conception of Islam and the Prophet in contemporary and later literature remained practically unchanged from the Medieval conception.[36] Muhammad was still the heretic and false Prophet, author of religion based on deceit. And these prejudices recur over and again. As Maxime Rodinson points out, the Western unfavorable image of Islam arose not only from hostile contact that accumulated over the centuries, but also from the inevitable distortions of the ideological rivalry of Christendom.[37] The ideological rivalry of the West led to a "brutally polemical image of a diabolical foe,"[38] an image that would both show the hateful nature of Islam by means of presenting it in unflattering terms and would also be such as to satisfy the literary taste for the exotic and the fabulous that had struck the Christian world in its dealings with the Muslims. The Muslim Orient was of interest not only from a theological and ideological point of view; it also exerted a public influence on the minds that longed for a strange and different culture. When A. Galland's translated version of the *Arabian Nights* appeared early in the eighteenth century (1704-17), Islamic material was no longer regarded as that of a distant, threatening foe; rather it was picturesque, something to delight a receptive audience,[39] a strange, curious matter, fascinating but inexplicable, so different that it is almost from another planet. But, while a romantic attitude starts to emerge, pushing religious matters to the background, the polemical image was still on the scene.

That the Western literary tradition accepted legends about the Muslims and their religion on face value and indulged in the use of related clichés proves to be unquestionable, but theological intolerance was also demonstrated in the wide range of works that examined the life of the Prophet. Lancelot Addison's biographical treatment of Muhammad, *First State of Muhametism, or an Account of the Author and Doctrine of that Imposture*, published anonymously in 1678, views that Prophet as a false messenger of God, and his doctrine as a heresy within Christianity characterized by force and deceit. The contemporary *True Nature of Imposture Fully Displayed in the Life of Mahomet* (1697), by Humphrey Prideaux, shows, as in the title, how the true nature of imposture is embodied in Islam, capitalizing on such theses as the sensuality of the Prophet, and emphasizing carnality as the first criterion of imposture. Later, in 1734, George Sale, in the hope of helping the church convert the Muslims to Christianity, translated the Qur'an into English directly from the Arabic. Sale in his introduction was the first to originate the view that the Qur'an is dull and repetitious and a manifest "forgery."[40] Other polemic works appeared about the same time as well.[41]

However, I shall now briefly survey the continuity of Oriental material in English literature, which provided themes for many writers famous and obscure alike, focusing particular attention on the romantic writers.[42] In the romantic era a different idea of the Muslim Orient, if somewhat reductionist, appeared alongside the well-established older image, largely, though not completely, displacing it. This is a period when almost all of the Muslim world was practically under Western domination, and Europe predominated. The growing power of the European naval strength increased East-West contact, and this contact in turn results in a massive influx of Oriental material into Western, particularly British, literature. Robert Southey's *Thalaba* (1801) provides a useful starting point. The poem involves a conflict between evil and good forces; the conflict consists of the attempts made by the witches to find and destroy, the representative of good, Thalaba, who is a devout Muslim, and of Thalaba's attempts to destroy the representative of evil, the Domdaniel. The members of Thalaba's family have been massacred by Okba, a Domdaniel Magician. Thalaba's quest drags him into a number of challenging adventures. Such a tale would seem to force Southey to present Islam, through Thalaba's search for the Domdaniel, as the good that is doomed to stand in the face of evil powers, but in fact Southey had no genuine sympathy with Islam. In his pursuit, Thalaba finally approaches Baghdad. At this point Southey breaks the course of the narrative, and delivers the following apostrophe:

> So one day may the Crescent from thy Mosques
> Be pluck'd by Wisdom, when the enlighten'd arm
> Of Europe conquers to redeem the East!
> (Book V. vi)[43]

The spirit of imperialistic zeal, which started to emerge at the time, is clear. But what should be clarified more here is that Thalaba's Muslim faith is inappropriate in the poem, and so is the divine protection he receives, since the superior arm of Europe will pluck the Crescent from the Mosques where Thalaba's faith is practised only to replace it with the redeeming Cross. In other words, Southey undermines the imaginative world that he is trying to create in failing to abandon his personal prejudices and chauvinism.

A revealing view of Southey's attitude toward Muhammad and Islam is found in a letter to John May dated July 29, 1799:

Of the few books with me I am most engaged by the Koran: it is dull and full of repetitions, but there is an interesting simplicity in the tenets it inculcates. What was Mohammed? Self-deceived, or knowingly a deceiver? If an enthusiast, the question again recurs, wherein does real inspiration differ from mistaken? This is a question that puzzles me, because to the individual they are the same, and both effects equally proceed from the first Impeller of all motions, who must have ordained whatever he permits. In this train of reasoning I suspect a fallacy, but cannot discover it. But of Mohammed, there is one fact which in my judgment stamps the imposter.... The huge and monstrous fables of Mohammedanism, his extravagant miracles, and the rabbinical tenets of his followers, appear no where in the written book [the Qur'an]. Admit the inspiration of the writer, and there is nothing to shock belief. There is but one God--this is the foundation; Mohammed is his prophet--this is the superstructure. His followers must have been miserably credulous. They gained a victory over the Koreish with very inferior numbers, and fought lustily for it. Yet Mohammed says, and appeals to them for the truth of what he says, that not they beat the Koreish, but three thousand angels won the victory for them. The system has been miserably perverted and fatally successful.[44]

Even though Southey seems to see in the Qur'an something reasonable (given the authenticity of inspiration), he suggests here that Islam as a developed religion of the world is a corruption of that reasonableness. This view would or could, I think, have some relevance to the world of *Thalaba*. Now Thalaba is chosen from the start by Allah to be the destroyer of evil, the Domdaniel. He has neither intellectual force, nor physical power. He is simply an immature young man whose strength lies in his faith (Islam), and with it only can he carry out the task of standing against the evil of the world as is embodied in the Domdaniel. But Southey, rather confusedly, undermines this sense of reasonableness he seems to find in Islam, both in the letter and the poem. He must have had no other choice but to agree, as the Christian polemicists asserted, that the Prophet was only an impostor as a prophet and that his claim to Prophethood can only be accepted as false.

When Southey's contemporary, Thomas Moore, wrote *Lalla Rookh* (1817), the vogue of Orientalism was at its peak. The idea of a glamorous Muslim Orient struck not only romantic writers, but also the audience that longed for the foreign and the exotic. *Lalla Rookh* is a sequence of four stories that are told by a poet, Feramorz: "The Veiled Prophet of Khorassan," "Paradise and the Peri," "The Fire Worshippers," and "The Light of the Haram." The Veiled Prophet, known as al-Mokanna (Arabic for "the Veiled") compares Zelika's position among his *harem* to Muhammad's coffin, which Moore suspends at Madinah:

> Half mistress and half saints, though hang'st as even
> As doth Medina's tomb, twixt hell and heaven.
> (p. 45)[45]

At the time common was the belief that the Prophet's tomb was suspended between the floor and the ceiling of the vault where he was buried (more often the tomb was thought to be in Makkah). And in a passage in the prose narrative typical legends about Muhammad and the Qur'an are implied. Muhammad's "Koran, too, supposed to be the identical copy between the leaves of which Mahomet's favorite pigeon used to nestle, had been mislaid by his Koran-bearer three whole days."[46] "Paradise and the Peri" is based on the Persian legend of the Peris, a breed of fallen angels, who are permitted all the kinds of delight of earth, but not that of Paradise. The Peri, however, may be forgiven if she brings a tear of a repentant sinner. Her task is done, and Paradise is finally won.

> And she already hears the trees
> of Eden, with their crystal bells
> Ringing in that ambrosial breeze
> That from the throne of Alla swells.
> (p. 150)

The description of Paradise is rather romantic, a description which is characterized by the fabulousness and the charm of exoticism of the "trees of Eden" and their "crystal bells" (Muslim Paradise is often viewed as sensual.) "The Fire-Worshippers" deals with the defeat of the Zoroastrians by the Muslims who invaded Persia. The Muslim emir who conquers Persia is described, in words that come oddly and queerly from Feramorz, the Muslim narrator, as

> One of that saintly, murd'rous brood,
> To carnage and the Koran given,

21

Who think through unbelievers' blood
Lies their directest path to heav'n;--
One, who will pause and kneel unshod,
In the warm blood his hand hath pour'd,
To mutter o'er some text of God
Engraven on his reeking sword.
                    (p. 175)

But Feramorz's censorious attitude toward Islam soon changes; in effect he gives his allegiance to Islam as soon as his task as a story teller is over. The poem offers no evidence to indicate what Moore's intention was. But it seems that such a transition in the narrative was part of Moore's plan for the work as a whole: to romanticize the Orient and make it a fabulous exotic theme.

Moore's friend, Lord Byron, actually went to the Near Orient. He traveled in Greece, Albania, and Turkey, "convinced of the advantages of looking at mankind instead of reading about them."[47] Upon his return to England he published his travel observations in the first two cantos of *Childe Harold's Pilgrimage* (1809-1818), which won him immediate recognition. *Childe Harold's Pilgrimage* capitalizes upon the Greek struggle against the Turks for freedom, which Byron conceives of as a struggle between Christianity and Islam. As might be expected, Byron would show much sympathy with the Christian Greeks and little admiration for the tyrannical Muslim Turks and their culture (the image of the Turk was still associated with tyranny and barbarism).

Land of Albania! let me bend mine eyes
On thee, thou rugged nurse of Savage Men!
The Cross descends, thy minarates arise,
And the pale Crescent sparkles in the glen.
                    (*CHP* II. 38)[48]

Byron's first hand observation in the Orient, however, enabled him to try his hand at another poem with Oriental background. In *The Giaour* (1813), a poem of love between a Venetian outlaw and a young Muslim damsel, Leila, Byron captures the spirit of the Muslim Orient and its people. In fact, despite his anti-Turk sentiments, he knew and imitated Oriental literature. Take, for example, the following passage in which the Muslim fisherman describes the scene the Giaour is looking at:

Why looks he o'er the olive wood?--
The crescent glimmers on the hill,
The Mosque's high lamps are quivering still;
Though too remote for sound to wake
In echoes of the far tophaike,
The flashes of each joyous peal
Are seen to prove the Moslem's zeal.
To-night--set Ramzani's sun--
To-night--the Bairam feast's begun--
                    (p. 47)

Apparently Byron not only used the word "Crescent" because it suggested Islam, but because the Crescent itself at the end of Ramadan is indeed a sign of the beginning of the Bairam feast, which is an occasion of joyous rejoicing, and the passage shows that he knew something of the Muslim calendar. And again, in describing Leila, the fisherman says:

Her eye's dark charm 'twere vain to tell,
But gaze on that of the Gazelle,
It will assist thy fancy well,
As large, as languishingly dark,
But soul beam'd forth in every spark
That darted from beneath the lid,
Bright as the jewel of Giamschid.
                    (p. 55)

Comparing a woman's eyes to those of a gazelle is commonly done in Arabic lite-rature, and the comparison of Leila's cheeks to "young pomegranate's blossom" (1. 494) is similarly characteristic of this literature. (Leila was the most famous female lover in Arabic and Persian literatures.) Byron might had borrowed such details from books and other sources, but even if he did they are revealing and show in-depth acquaintance with the Muslim Near Orient and its culture on Byron's part.

With the end of the British romantic era the Muslim Orient had long become a setting for what Edward Said, in his pioneering work on the subject, has called "Orientalism."[49] For, argues C.H. Becker, "as the West emerges from the shadow-land of the Middle Ages the more definite becomes its superiority over the East. Western nationals become convinced that the fetters which bind them were forged in the East, and when they have shaken off their chains, they discover their own physical and intellectual power. They go forth and create a new world, in which Orientalism finds but a scanty room."[50]

That the West's superiority over the East becomes "more definite," at least on the material level, we know. But we cannot find any period since the Crusades in which the Muslim Orient was presented outside a framework created by Orientalism, which finds a tremendously vast room in the Western literary tradition, let alone other traditions. Orientalism, suggests Said, is ultimately a cultural doctrine willed over the Orient because the Orient becomes inferior to the West; this doctrine forced a "difference between the familiar (Europe, the West, 'us') and the strange (the Orient, the East, 'them')."[51] So the Orientalist makes the Orient speak, using a generality of labels like "the Muslim", "the Arab" versus "the Westerner." In any event, the imbalance between the Muslim East and the Christian West remains obviously a function of changing cultural and historical patterns.

Little of the Oriental material encountered in the European, especially the British, literatures is to be found in America's literary experience of the Muslim and non-Muslim East. American contact with the Muslim Orient was very limited; we can only think of occasional travelers like John L. Stephens, George W. Curtis, Bayard Taylor, Mark Twain, and Melville, or of minor religious missions, or of naval and military expeditions against the Barbary pirates, or of the transcendentalists who saw affinities between Indian thought and their own. Admittedly, there was no culmination or concreteness of Orientalism in American literature. But, in their turn, Americans, for obvious links of language and culture, took over the older attitudes of cultural hostility and unwittingly kept them. And American literature reflects this by generally perpetuating the firmly established stereotypes and images.

Late in the eighteenth century American literary magazines carried such Oriental tales as exotic as "Bathmendi" (1787), "Salyma and Ossmin" (1788), "Omar and Fatima" (1807),[52] and Benjamin Franklin wrote such shorter works as "A Narrative of the Late Massacres..." (1764), "An Arabian Tale" (1779), and "On the Slave Trade" (1790).[53] But the Barbary Wars (1785-1815) were the first actual encounter between the Muslim Orient and the young American republic, marking the initial important impact of the Muslim East on American culture and literature, and the "Barbary pirates" affair virtually sums up what Americans most knew of the Muslim World until the 1970s, the Arab-Israeli wars, the Palestine Liberation Organization, and the Organization of Petroleum Exporting Countries. In their perception of the Barbary wars, American writers generally relied on traditional European views and Stereotypes. These wars furnished the themes of such works as Susanna Rowson's *Slaves in Algiers* (1794), Royall Tyler's *The*

Algerine Captive (1797), John Howard Payne's *Fall of Algiers* (1826?), Richard Penn Smith's *The Bombardment of Algiers* (1829), Joseph Stenvens Jones' *The Usurper* (1841), and other contemporary literature that generally presented a reductionist view of North African privateering and a horrific image of "the Barbary", exaggerated and enlarged.[54]

Royall Tyler's *The Algerine Captive* is an obvious example of the Barbary-oriented American literature. The work consists of two volumes: the first presents a colorful picture of American life; and the second, while concentrating on Algerine society, life, and beliefs, presents a nationalistic perception of the alien. *The Algerine Captive* is essentially a continuation of the captivity narrative,[55] which goes back to the early colonial period, the mid-seventeenth century. Updike Underhill's narrative implies a metaphorical process of creating a genuinely American mythology that suggests patriotic zeal. Given its thematic suggestiveness in the book, captivity is not, however, a central theme. For *The Algerine Captive* is also a travel narrative, and Underhill is the first American innocent abroad who wants to provide the American reader with fabulous information about the Barbary states, the Muslim East, the Barbary Prophet, and the Algerian social life in general, among other things Islamic.

The first volume of *The Algerine Captive* covers Underhill's trip aboard the American vessel *Freedom*, which is bound for Africa to bring slaves. From the very outset, Underhill's sympathy with the slaves, and thus antipathy to the horror of slavery, is revealed. When one of the Negro slaves befriends him, Underhill exclaims: "Is this one of those men whom we are taught to vilify as beneath the human species?"[56] When Underhill himself is taken into captivity by the Algerines and sold as a slave, he realizes more acutely the values of freedom (even the ship's name becomes symbolic of these values), but his conception of such values is both patriotic and nationalistic. Underhill says:

> It was amidst the parched sands and flinty rocks of Africa that thou [i.e., God] taughtest me that the bread was indeed pleasant, and the water sweet. Let those of our fellow citizens who set at nought the rich blessings of our Federal union go like me to a land of slavery and they will then learn to appreciate the value of our free government.
> (p. 132)

In these circumstances Underhill, as he tells us in the Preface, would be able to "display a portrait [not only] of New England manners, hitherto unattempted," but also those "of that ferocious race [the Algerian Muslims], so dreaded by commercial powers, and so little known in our country" (pp. 28-29). Thus Underhill has the advantage of examining the American perception of the outside world, particularly a world as foreign as that of the Algerians.

In doing so, Underhill becomes aware that "it is the privilege of travelers to exaggerate; but," he adds, "I wish not to avail myself of this prescriptive right. I had rather disappoint the curiosity of my readers by conciseness, than disgust them with untruths. I have no ambition to be ranked among the Bruces and Chastelleaux of the age. I shall therefore endeavour rather to improve the under-standing of my reader, with what I really know, than amuse him with stories of which my circumscribed situation rendered me necessarily ignorant" (p. 177). How far from exaggeration Underhill is has to be assessed.

Well on his way to Madinah, having passed through Arabia Petraea, Underhill, Tyler's "author," tells us of "Many a dreadful story" which his fellow travelers (not he) asserted. They told of "poisonous winds and overwhelming sands, and of the fierce wandering Arabs who captured whole caravans and ate their prisoners. Many a bloody battle had they fought with this cruel banditti, in which, according to their narratives, they always came off conquerors"(p. 211). The marvelous, the exotic, and the fabulous go hand in hand with the weird. For it was the common tradition of many travelers, whether real or fictitious, to report a preconceived picture; what their readers wanted to read, not what they actually saw or observed. And the result is not only a distorted image that the readers gain, but an unsympathetic understanding of the Muslim Orient as well.

While defending the verity of the Christian creed against "so detestably ridiculous a system as the Mahometan imposture" (p. 135), Underhill indulges in a series of arguments about the two faiths. In the dialogue between enslaved Underhill and the Muslim Mullah (or priest) attention is immediately drawn to the Prophet and the Qur'an. The dialogue runs thus:

Author. "You speak well. I will bring my religion to the test. Compare it with the --the--"

Mollah. "Speak out boldly. No advantage shall be taken. You would say, with the mahometan imposture. To determine which of the two revealed religions is best, two inquiries are alone necessary. First which of them has the highest proof of its divine origin? And second, which inculcates the purest morals? That is, of which have we the greatest certainty that it came from God, and which is calculated to do most good to mankind?

Author. "True. As to the first point, our Bible was written by men divinely inspired."

Mollah. "Our Alcoran was written by the figure of the Deity himself. But who told you your Bible was written by men divinely inspired?"

Author. "We have received it from our ancestors, and we have as good evidence of the truths it contains as we have in profane history for any historical fact."

Mollah. "And so we have the Alcoran. Our sacred and profane writers all prove the existence of such a prophet as Mahomet...."

Author. "We know the Christian religion is true from its small beginnings and wonderful increase...." The dialogue continues:

Author. "Our religion was disseminated in peace; yours was promulgated by the sword."

Mollah. "My friend you surely have not read the writings of your own historians. The history of the Christian church is a detail of bloody massacre...."

Author. "But you hold a sensual paradise."

Mollah. "So the doctors of your church tell you...."

Drawing a parallel which criticizes Christianity too, Underhill allows the Mullah to defend Islam against Christian charges. But at the end, having drawn this parallel between the two religions, Underhill, "disgusted with [the Mullah's] fables" (p. 143), decides to dismiss the entire argument as invalid. Even though such questions as the belief in God, the Scriptures, and the Prophets cut across both religions, the fact remains (given the irony of this fiction) that Underhill was better qualified to judge Christianity than Islam.

Back home Underhill declares: "I now mean ... to contribute cheerfully to the support of our excellent government which I have learnt to adore in the schools of depotism.... My ardent wish is that my fellow citizens may profit by my misfortunes" (p. 224). Such a statement obviously implies little more than nationalism; it suggests the superiority and integrity of the American political institution and morale that Underhill represents as an American citizen.

As I have suggested, Americans first met the Muslim Orient through the Tripolitanian Wars waged to put an end to the capture of American sailors by the Barbary pirates from the coastal areas of North Africa. This Barbary-oriented American literature, consisting mainly of captivity reports, travel narratives, and a few novels and plays, introduced Americans to the Muslim East. Royall Tyler's *The Algerine Captive* had reported exhaustively on the pirates, their habits, customs, history, and religion as we have seen. And cruel Barbary despots provided savage villains most foul for popular literature of the period and struck the

27

imagination of an appreciative public. Treatments of the Barbary idea mingled excitement and adventure to form a grim stereotype of the Barbary, in which ferocity was the common theme. There are historical and cultural reasons for this stereotype, of course, and from stereotype to myth-making the steps being slippery, Americans quickly made the descent. Richard Penn Smith's *The Bombardment of Algiers* (1829), an unplayed melodrama preserved by the Historical Society of Pennsylvania, and Joseph Stenvens Jones's *The Usurper: or Americans in Tripoli* (1841) are an obvious precursor.

Richard Penn Smith (1799-1854), author of *The Bombardment of Algiers*, a Philadelphia lawyer and playwright wrote as many as twenty plays, thirteen of which were based on French sources.[57] Two of Smith's earliest manuscripts, both dated 1825, are *The Pelican*, a one-act farce which was neither performed nor printed, and *The Divorce*, a weak attempt at romantic comedy founded on French inspiration. Four years later, in 1829, Smith's activity as a dramatist was at its peak. In that year, he wrote six plays: *The Eighth of January; The Disowned; A Wife at a Venture; The Sentinels, or the Two Sergeants; William Penn;* and *The Bombardment of Algiers*, all lost manuscripts, published only in 1940, under the auspices of the Dramatists' Guild of the Authors' League of America. Among these plays *The Bombardment of Algiers* is alone based on Barbary inspiration, a non-native, far-fetched influence that never fails to show its presence.

The play opens with a dialogue between two gardeners of the Dey of Algiers. In a coarse tone the Muslim Barbuctar, somewhat oddly, asks the Christian Benjamin for some wine, and drinks to the health of the Prophet, while telling Benjamin to "let Mahomet alone!" Though the drunkard is reminded by Benjamin: "Your creed tells you that you will go to the devil if you drink in this manner," he goes on drinking, the pleasures of which he prefers to the demands of faith (Islam), pronouncing it "A very pleasant way of going to the devil".[58] Benjamin finally gives himself up to drunkenness as well. His motive in not wanting Barbuctar to do so is because he does not want to appear before the Cadi (the judge) accused of giving wine to a Muslim. But he has dared to purvey wine among the Muslims, despite a punishment that has once been inflicted upon him, thus ironically ignoring profane law and religious creeds alike. Benajmin and Barbuctar have to appear before the Cadi, and there is no sin more agreeable and more innocent than the selling and drinking of wine in a Muslim country! Himself drunk, the chief of the eunuchs, Nilouf, outrageously declares: "When the Prophet proscribed wine, he left his followers nothing half as good to moisten their clay with" (p. 35). In this ironic situation, the two gardeners are soon freed. For that hated liquor has, regardless of all religious restrictions and beliefs, worked its way through the Dey's Court itself. Nothing can be more ironic and grotesque in this regard.

In the meantime, however, the French are disposed to attack Algiers to free French slaves. They have a considerable fleet at sea, determined not to quit until it has entirely destroyed the country. The melodramatic dialogue between Benjamin and Barbuctar recognizes no such devastation as war, however. In addition to wine, the subject-matter of the dialogue concerns itself with Benjamin himself. We learn that Benajmin Hardy, now a French slave in Algiers, has been taken into captivity together with his master, the Chevalier de Choiseuil, and both suffer miserably when they are sold to a Barbary corsair, from whom Barbuctar rescues them. Benjamin pathetically recalls: "I beheld five or six of those rascals [i.e., Algerines], who attacked me and carried me, neck and heels, on board their vessel" (p. 37). Barbuctar's sympathy for enslaved Benjamin and antipathy to the horror of human slavery are soon revealed when he vows: "I will struggle to ... prove that under the burning sun of Africa and in the country that they call barbarous, there are faithful hearts that acknowledge the laws of gratitude" (p. 37).

The dialogue then invites our attention to the Dey of Algiers, Ismael Mezamorte, who falls in love with the charm and beauty of Valentine, Choiseuil's enslaved wife, who is in the Dey's harem at Dessra. Her charm has conquered Ismael, and she supplants the beautiful Zamira, who has so long kept possession of the Dey's heart. Ismael acknowledges: "I have indulged in the pleasures which my harem [i.e., Christian Valentine and Muslim Zamira] presented to me, and totally neglected the cares of the government" (p. 38). Thus, confined to eternal slavery, helpless Valentine will be nothing more than a sensual amusement to the Dey's lust. A man who neglects the cares of an infirm, insecure government for love and voluptuousness and who obliges a woman-slave to love him by force must, of course, be a barbarian. The character of the Dey, dating back to the Middle Ages, recalls the view that the Muslims are "intensely emotional and excitable people.... always going from one emotional extreme to another. Socially, they are the embodiment of all foul practices. Thus they use slaves, they beat their prisoners, they buy and sell their womenfolk, and they practise polygamy".[59] In the play, the Dey is always to be found in the midst of the harem, with its beautiful gardens, vases and temples with enslaved *houris* amusing or applying themselves in various amusements, some delightful ways. Even the heavenly paradise of Eden cannot be more charming and enchanting. The eunuch of the harem, Osmin, tells us that Valentine appears "before the women of the harem with all the eclat that becomes the mistress of [Ismael's] heart" (p. 54). Valentine does appear before the Dey's harem during a fête bestowed with all the glamour that Ismael's fantasies can imagine, only to reign over the heart of the passionate Dey.

Filled with remorse for his failure to run his failing government, Ismael admits: "Seduced by pleasure, I listened to the insidious tongues of those by whom I was surrounded. They have deceived me. I believed you were happy, and misery had overtaken you. At length I have rent asunder the veil that concealed your grievances; at length truth breaks upon me and will prove that I am worthy of the trust reposed in me." Ismael's admission clearly turns into self-accusation at this point, suggesting a bitter recognition that he is neither a sovereign, nor is he worthy of reverence at all. For he has wilfully neglected a government to win the heart of an attractive slave. Even his subjects are no more lucky than Valentine; they are oppressed people and their grievances hardly reach their Dey's ears. In brief, Ismael has turned himself into a fearful tyrant, who has done nothing for the welfare of his people. Malpractice and injustice are practised in his name instead. Rather than proving himself worthy of the trust reposed in him as a Dey, Ismael falls victim to the irreconcilable conflict between sensual pleasures and the highly demanding duties of a Dey of the State of Algiers. Filled with a wild, unreasoning love for French Valentine the Dey shows his infatuation thus: "Lonely Valentine, at length I see you within a palace where a sovereign is your slave. Here all things combine to render your life happy, and your lot will be enviable indeed if you are not insensible to that love with which *your charms have inspired me*" (p. 58).[60] For a Dey like Ismael to be a slave in the name of wild passion falls far beyond any stretch of the imagination. But Ismael does it, and does it willingly.

The French fleet is now menacing Algiers, determined to attack Ismael's states. But Ismael can neither obtain peace nor save his people. He has no choice other than dishonour or death. He would not himself hesitate to defend his power to the last extremity, but his oppressed subjects would undoubtedly fail him in fighting the redoubtable Christian enemy, France. Convinced that a king cannot dishonour himself when he prefers the well-being of his subjects to his personal glory, Ismael proposed peace to the French admiral, "Christian, why am I at war with your nation?" enquires Ismael, "I don't hesitate to avow that the character of France has always inspired me with the highest esteem. Your bravery and your conduct ... convince me that you deserve my confidence, and I am ready to give you a proof of it" (p. 61). To prevent a possible war he is ready to release all the French captives (yet there is no mention of the beloved Valentine). But should the French admiral turn Ismael's offer down, Ismael will justifiably resort to war: "I will bury myself with the last of my subjects beneath the ruins of this town," Ismael asserts, "and I will not perish without drawing with me some of my enemies" (p. 62). Alas, the French fleet appears at the entrance of the port of

30

Dessra and the thunders of the French artillery shake Ismael's ramparts. Algiers is besieged, "the soldiers swear, the women cry, and the children scream and bawl" (p. 70) and Ismael is left all alone in an abject situation in the hour of utmost need. The danger and fury of war press more and more only to enflame the rage of helpless Ismael. Fortunately, if surprisingly, the French do accept the Dey's proposition of peace in the end. Valentine is finally freed and reunited with her dear husband, Choiseuil, who brings news of peace to the terrified Ismael. Happily, Valentine is in actuality no longer in Ismael's power; Ismael has freed her and, as it should seem, he could not have shown her greater kindness. Had it not been for the use of force, the Dey would not have been so benevolent.

Twelve years later, in 1841, Joseph Stenvens Jones, a Boston actor, and author of more than 150 melodramas, farces, and comedies, contributed to American drama *The Usurper: or Americans in Tripoli*, set, as the title reveals, in the Barbary Orient. As playwright, Jones' reputation was so high that the manager of New York's Bowery Theatre opened in 1841 (the year Jones wrote *The Usurper*) with the proud declaration that he had engaged as dramatist J.S. Jones of Boston. Jones graduated at Harvard in 1843 as a Doctor of Medicine, and, until his death in 1877, he practiced medicine occasionally, delivered lectures on anatomy and physiology, and was often referred to by acquaintances as "the celebrated Dr. Jones." Typical of its author's melodramatic style, patriotic enthusiasm, and love of the outlandish is The *Usurper*.[61]

The play informs us at the outset that the Dey of Algiers, proud and arrogant Abdel Mahadi, now sits on a throne he has usurped from a worthy brother, Ali Ben Mahadi, "revelling in the wealth he forces from the good people of Tripoli who dare not murmur of the extortion".[62] The play reveals the exactions and tyranny of Abdel Mahadi, who, by false accusations, banishes his brother from Tripoli to seize a throne he is unworthy of. The usurper metes out "oppression and death to all who dare to thwart his will" (p. 151). He is a very ambitious monarch indeed, and brings to mind another Ismael, different though his person seems to be. We first meet Abdel Mahadi in all his magnificence in a splendid palace in the suburbs of Tripoli. The following is what he has to say:

> O rapturous thought! I, who for years have pined in blank
> obscurity, have, like the ravenous tiger, overleaped the
> ignominious bound and poured destruction on the wretch
> who rashly dared to check my will. Now shall the darling
> passion of my soul be glutted. Plunder! Aye, plunder alone
> can raise our sinking realm. Peace has no charms for me; her

train is misery and want. Plunder shall fill our coffers and once more give to Tripoli happiness and fame (pp. 153-54).

Abdel Mahadi becomes a glutton for plunder, thriving on ravage and devastation. For in his eyes "plunder alone can raise [his] sinking realm" and fill his heart with rapture. Such a man neither knows peace nor is himself peaceful. Plunder alone can grant him the happiness and fame he seeks. He overleaps "the ignominious bound and poured destruction" on his subjects good and bad alike. Even when it comes to so close a being as a brother, Abdel Mahadi does not have the slightest hesitation in commanding the soldiery to point their sabres at his brother's guilt-less heart, reporting lies of foulest import, and charging innocent Ali Ben Mahadi with treason till he comes to the throne he knows he does not deserve. Indeed the usurper is the "most ill-natured, malicious, good-for-nothing creature" (p. 158) than whom no man can be more disgraceful!

If the French fleet eventually forces the threatened Ismael to accept peace, Americans undertake the same role in avenging their national morale and integrity. For in the play a ship with full cargo from America has been taken into captivity by the Barbary corsairs. Seated on a throne surrounded by officers, guards, slaves, male and female dancers, Abdel Mahadi speaks: "these Christian dogs shall feel my deadly hate" (p. 154). Dialogue between him and an American captive, soon reveals that he is less demanding in fact. Abdel Mahadi desires to know whether America will ransom her captives in Tripoli. The troubled Mahadi is stunned to find out "that the only ransom [Tripoli] will get from America for [American prisoners] will be in iron balls in the shape of forty-two pounders. That will make your Deyship tremble" (p. 157). The threat makes Mahadi tremble at the certainty of war if he does not set his captives at liberty immediately.

In the meantime the American captives await their country's boasted vengeance, implying patriotic zeal and suggesting the superiority of the American political institution that the captives represent. They now know more acutely the values of freedom, and their conception of such values is both patriotic and zealous. They want to contribute enthusiastically to the support of their government which they have learnt to adore more in the Barbary land of despotism. One captive assures himself and his fellow Americans: "We ain't going to surrender to these copper-coloured swabs [i.e. the Algerines] without firing a shot, eh! No, shiver my timbers if we do. So stand by, my hearties, and we'll pour in a broadside for the honour of our country and ourselves" (p. 157). Now the situation is that these American captives of Tripoli, civilized, polished, and brave, end up seeking liberty from savage, wild, and barbarious Arabs (p. 160). So the Barbary Orient is given here a space where it stands vis-à-vis the Occident, setting up certain boundaries and categories and making cultural, if not racial, distinctions.

This is a more revealing view of American zeal. Edward Anderson, an American sailor and captive in Tripoli, pathetically wonders:

> Oh, what a change is here! Yesterday! What was I yesterday? Opulent and free. Today! today! A beggar and a slave! O my countrymen! Where now that Roman pride, that Spartan valour, that enthusiastic zeal, which led you on to freedom and to glory, that here, in this vile nest of pirates, beneath a sun whose pestilential rays spread death around, thy fellow countrymen must bend like overburdened beasts, with slavery and shame (p. 161).

Speaking out of nationalistic pride and zeal, Anderson and his fellow Americans feel assured of regaining their liberty; their country will avenge their captivity and put an end to this "vile nest of pirates." Obviously Anderson is concerned here with the sordid problems unjustly created by North African Piracy, and his concern stems mainly from a sense of high glory. Piracy has given up these Americans, Anderson included of course, into the hands of the fierce and barbarous monsters of Africa who have oppressed their captives with a slavery wherein they bend with dishonour and shame. But an awareness of America's determination and ability to "blow Algiers to the devil" (p. 161) never abandons these Americans. The Americans recount their sufferings and grievances as captives in Tripoli, yet never do they lose hope of victory over the man who has harmed them, the base usurper.

A frigate bearing the American flag and several other large vessels of war finally arrive off Tripoli to demand of the Dey the release of all American prisoners without a ransom. This daring act suggests the same force of the French fleet which obliged Ismael Mezamorte to consider peace under the threat artillery. Worse, towards the end of the play Mahadi gets a report that the Americans desire to reinstate his brother, who now heads an army to meet Mahadi's force. Ali Ben Mahadi is confident that "with this powerful assistance [of the US navy], we cannot fail of success. Victory will be ours, and my vanquished brother must sue to me for pardon" (p. 169). The Americans promise that Ali Ben Mahadi will be reinstated on condition that the American captives are immediately released and their plundered property restored. Ali Ben Mahadi fulfills the American demands diligently in fighting against his brother's tyranny and oppression in the name of liberty. He actually attacks Tripoli, and a general bombardment takes place, leaving the city in ruins. Ali and Mahadi fight face to face in the end and it is the freed Edward Anderson who strikes the usurper dead. Thus America is victorious, and the American flag is hoisted.

Smith's *The Bombardment of Algiers* and Jones' *The Usurper,* uphold, among other things, American national honour and pride, for which the Orient has to pay a costly price; in one case in morale, in the other in life itself. Following these early nineteenth century stereotypes of the Muslim Barbary Orient, are numerous later sources with Barbary themes. Such books as Edith Wharton's *In Morocco* (1920), Ernest Hemingway's *The Green Hills of Africa* (1935), Kenneth Roberts' *Lydia Bailey* (1947), Norman Mailer's *The Barbary Shore* (1951), and Violet Winspear's *The Sheik's Captive* (1979) continue and reiterate the idea of a Muslim Barbary Orient up to our own day. These representations, ideas, and images have been reiterated so frequently in American writing, popular and otherwise, that they have become the reflection of reality for most readers. The impact of certain ideas has in effect been particularly pervasive because there are few works in which the Orient is depicted in favourable terms.

Suffice it to say, then, that Western attitudes toward Islam followed certain themes which relate to religion, power, and sexual laxity. These themes are in effect the traditional areas of polemic against Islam. For centuries the West tended to view Islam as a corrupt religion based on false beliefs. The change of opinion in these themes from the eleventh century to the nineteenth was slight. There were some changes of detail, of course, but this attitude remained in the background. The medieval Christian West was culturally inferior to its contemporary rival, the Muslim East; but at the end of the Ottoman period the West equaled and even surpassed Islam, both on the military and cultural levels. With the rise in power, the West's penetration of the Muslim world forced it to form new views. But the new came alongside the traditional conflict of ideas between the two worlds. The traditional attitudes constituted the background of the actual experience of the Muslim Orient by Europeans and Americans. Thus a few American authors in the nineteenth century, famous and obscure alike, conveyed traditional prejudice and misinformation in their writings. And my purpose is to identify and distinguish these prejudices and to see what Islam and the Muslims meant to Americans. With this literary and cultural background, it is the business of the following chapter to examine Washington Irving's conceptions of the mystery and romantic suggestiveness of Muslim Spain.

Notes

1 By the Muslim East I mean the area from Turkey on the Black Sea southwards through Syria, Jordan, Saudi Arabia, and Egypt back along the coastal lands of North Africa and up through Muslim Spain. This definition implies ideological rather than geographical associations; ideological in that it involves more historical, religious, and cultural issues than geographical. The terms "Orient" and "East" will be used interchangeably throughout this work.

2 See W. Montgomery Watt, *Islam and Christianity Today* (London: Routeledge and Kegan Paul, 1983), p. 4.

3 I shall adopt the modern and more accurate spelling in such words as Muhammad, Qur'an, Muslim, etc.

4 See Watt, *Islam and Christianity Today*, pp. 4-6

5 See "The Conventional Saracen of the Song of Geste," *Speculum* 17 (1942): 202.

6 Southern, *Western Views of Islam in the Middle Ages* (Cambridge: Harvard University Press, 1962).

7 *Ibid.*, p. 17

8 Dorothee Metlitzki Finkelstein, *The Matter of the Araby in Medieval England* (New Haven: Yale University Press, 1961), p. 3.

9 See Benjamin Kedar, *Crusade and Mission: European Approaches toward the Muslims* (Princeton: Princeton University Press, 1984), p. 45. Also see, for a general background, Jonathan Riley-Smith's *What Were the Crusades?* (London: MacMillan, 1977).

10 See James T. Addison, *The Christian Approach to the Moslem* (New York: Columbia University Press, 1942), p. 35.

11 George Sale, trans., *The Koran: Commonly Called the Alcoran of Mohammed*, 6th ed. (1734; rpt. Philadelphia: Lippincott and Co., 1876).

12 See John W. Voorhis, "John of Damascus on the Moslem Heresy," *Muslim World* 24 (Oct. 1934): 391-398.

13 See John W. Voorhis, "The Discussion of a Christian and a Saracen," *Muslim World* 25 (July 1935): 266-273.

14 *The Christian Approach to the Moslem*, p. 28.

15 See Dana C. Munro, "The Western Attitude toward Islam During the Period of the Crusades," *Speculum* VI, no. 3 (1931): 329-343.

16 See Philip Hitti, *Islam and the West* (Princeton, N.J.: D. Van Nostrand Co., 1962), p 52.

17 Norman Daniel, *Islam and the West* (Edinburgh: Edinburgh University Press, 1960), p. 1.

18 *Ibid.*, p. 68.

19 The degree of accuracy attempted by most medieval writers may be symbolized by the different forms in which the name of the prophet appears in the literature of the period. Maphomet, Baphometh, Mathomus, Malphus, Malphumeth, Mahummeth, Maehumeth, Mahomet, Mahound, and so forth.

20 See Byron Smith, *Islam in English Literature* (Beirut: American Press, 1939), pp. 6-7.

21 "The Conventional Saracen of the Song of Geste," *Speculum* 17 (1942): 203.

22 *Ibid.*, pp. 204-205.

23 *The Inferno of Dante*, trans. Lacy Lockert (Princeton: Princeton University Press, 1959). All references in the text follow this translation.

24 J.S.P. Tatlock, "Mohammed and His Followers in Dante," *MLR* 276 (1932): 192.

25 References in the text follow *The Song of Roland,* transl. D.D.R. Owen (London: George Allen and Unwin Ltd., 1972).

26 *Poem of the Cid,* trans. Rita Hamilton and Janet Perry (Manchester: Manchester University Press, 1975).

27 John Lydgate, *Fall of Princes*, ed. Henry Bergen (London: EETS, Extra Ser., no. 123, 1924), Pt. III, BK. IX, pp. 920-23.

28 Louis Wann has surveyed the Elizabethan plays which are based on Oriental themes. Wann remarks that forty-seven plays with such themes were written between 1558 and 1642. He suggests that, for many Elizabethans, the Orient was a "domain where war, conquest, fratricide, lust, and treachery had freer play than in the lands nearer home." See "The Oriental in Elizabethan Drama," *MP* 12 (1915): 423-47.

29 *The Works of Francis Bacon* (London: H. Bryer, 1803), II, 279.

30 Myron P. Gilmore, *The World of Humanism, 1453-1517* (New York: Harper and Row, 1952), pp. 20, 21.

31 See Robert Schoebel, *The Shadow of the Crescent: The Renaissance Image of the Turk* (Nieuwkoop, 1967). The book examines the Western attitude toward the Ottoman Turks in the critical years 1453-1517. It is essentially concerned with the forms and content of European thought on the subject.

32 Paul Coles, *The Ottoman Impact on Europe* (New York: Harcourt, Brace, and World, 1968), pp. 145-147.

33 Smith, p. 17.

34 *1 Tamburlaine The Great*, ed. J.S. Cunningham (Manchester University Press, 1981),III, iii, 46. Other references hereon refer to this edition.

35 *2 Tamburlaine*, V, i, 172-175.

36 One obvious example is John Dryden's *Don Sebastian* (1691), a tragicomedy based on a series of contrasts between the Christians and the Muslims. Muley-Moluch, the Muslim Emperor is, for instance, presented as a "shining ... character of brutality" (Preface, p. 289); Sebastian, King of Portugal, is, on the other hand, presented as "brave, pious, generous, great, and liberal" (I. i. 103). Other contrasts between Muslim and Christian characters in the play are generally in favor of the Christians. Reference is to *Four Tragedies*, ed. L.A. Beaurline and Fredson Bowers (Chicago: University of Chicago Press, 1967). See, for more detailed analysis, Byron Smith, especially pp. 47-52.

37 See, on this point, *The Legacy of Islam*, ed. Joseph Schacht, 2nd ed. (London: Oxford University Press, 1974), pp. 9-62.

38 *Ibid.*, p. 23.

39 *Ibid.*, p. 36.

40 Sale, *The Koran*, p.v. I should point out here that Sale's version of the Qur'an was preceded by a lesser known translation made by Alexander Ross, published in London in 1649, entitled "A needful Caveat or Admonition, for them who desire to know what use may be made of, or if there be danger in reading the Alcoran."

41 Such works include, as examples, Simon Ockley's *History of the Saracens* (1708-1718), Edward Gibbon's *The Decline and Fall of the Roman Empire* (1788), and Voltaire's *Le Fanatisme, ou Mahomet le Prophet* (1742).

42 See Martha P. Conant's *The Oriental Tale in England in the Eighteenth Century* (New York: Columbia University Press, 1908), and Marie E.

Meester's *Oriental Influences in the English Literature of the Nineteenth Century* (Heidelberg, 1915), for an overview of the subject.

43 Robert Southey, vol. 4 of *The Poetical Works* (London: Longman, Brown, and Green, 1838).

44 See *Selections from the Letters of Robert Southey*, ed. John Wood Warter (London: Longman, Brown and Green, 1856), I, 77-78.

45 *Lalla Rookh* (London: Longman, Hurst, and Brown, 1817).

46 *Ibid.*, p. 124.

47 Byron's *Works: Letters and Journals*, ed. Rowland E. Prothero (London: John Murray, 1898-1901), I, 309.

48 *The Complete Poetical Works*, ed. Jerome J. McGann (London: Oxford University Press, 1980), II, 56. References in the text refer to this edition.

49 See *Orientalism* (1978; rpt. New York: Vintage Books, 1979). The book offers an intelligent discussion of the word (Orientalism) as a body of ideas, beliefs, and clichés about the Muslim Near Orient.

50 C.H. Becker and H.J. Chaytor, *Christianity and Islam* (New York: B. Franklin Press, 1974), p. 104.

51 *Orientalism*, p. 43.

52 "Bathmendi," *The Columbian Magazine* 1 (Jan.-Feb., 1787): 246-292; "Salyma and Ossmin," *The American Magazine* (May-June, 1788): 363-439; "Omar and Fatima," *The Literary Magazine and American Register* 8 (1808): 5-301.

53 One of the earliest Americans to show awareness of the Muslim Orient is Cotton Mather. He was concerned with the problems created for Americans by North African piracy and with the religious missions into the Orient. Here is how Mather, reviewing the difficulties of New England, showed concern as early as 1702:

> ... In the midst of these deplorable things God had given up several of our sons into the hands of the fierce monsters of Africa. Mahometan Turks, and Moors, and devils, are at this day oppressing many of our sons with a *slavery* wherein they "wish for death, and cannot find it;" a slavery from where they cry and write unto us, "it had been good for us that we had never been born."

> (*Magnalia* [Hartford, 1854], II, 671)

Moved by the reports of captives who had become "Turk", Mather employed his "knowledge" of Islam in a work he intended to distribute to the Barbary Coast, *A Pastoral Letter to the English Captives in Africa* (1698). He advised these captives to exploit the Qur'an in defense of their creed:

> If any *Mahometan* Tempters do assault you, Let the words of their own *Alcoran* serve to Answer them; The words of the *Alcoran*, (Or Turkish Bible) are: *The Spirit of God hath given Testimony, to Christ, the Son of Mary; He is the Messenger of the Spirit, and the Word of God: His Doctrine is perfect.* And *Mahomet*, in his *Alcoran*, call the Gospel expressly, The Right way to Fear God; and says, *That God sent the Gospel for no other end, but that they might obtain by it, the Love and Grace of God.*

The above passage is quoted in Mukhtar Ali Isani's "Cotton Mather and the Orient," *New England Quarterly* 43 (March-Dec., 1970): 52-53. See, however, the whole article for a discussion of Mather's Oriental interests, pp. 46-58.

54 See, for a careful examination, Lotfi Ben Rejeb's "'to the Shores of Tripoli': The Impact of Barbary on Early American Nationalism". Diss. Indiana University 1981.

55 See, on this point, Roy Harvey Pearce, "The Significance of Captivity Narrative," *American Literature* 19 (1947) : 1-20.

56 Royall Tyler, *The Algerine Captive* (New Haven, Conn.: College and University Press, 1970), p. 118. Subsequent references in the text follow this edition.

57 Information on Smith is scanty and widely scattered. But such sources as *The Dictionary of American Biography* (New York, 1993) and Bruce Welker McCullough's *The Life and Writings of Richard Penn Smith* (Wisconsin, 1917) are very useful.

58 Quotations hereon are from *America's Lost Plays*, Vol. 13, ed. Ralph H. Ware and H.W. Schoenberger (Bloomington, 1965), p. 33, and below.

59 Quoted in Meredith Jones's "The Conventional Saracen of the Song of Geste," *Speculum* 17 (1942): 205..

60 Author's italics.

61 The title of the play bears the statement that *The Usurper* is "altered and compressed into three acts," I may only conclude here that this is Jones's revision of Smith's *The Bombardment of Algiers*. The names of characters differ obviously, but the controlling idea of bravery and patriotism in the face of abject Barbary hardships is the same.

62 Quotations hereon are from *America's Lost Plays*, vol. 14, p. 151.

But what do I want to drag myself around the Orient for, anyway? What do I care about these withered fragments of old orders, these dead religions, these ruins swarming with the maggots of history?

John Dos Passos, *Orient Express*

I began with the Mahommedan religion as being that with which I was then best acquainted myself, and of which everyone who had read the *Arabian Nights' Entertainments* possessed all the knowledge necessary for readily understanding and entering into the intent and spirit of the poem....

When I took up, for my next subject, that mythology...
I soon perceived that the best mode of treating it would be to construct a story altogether mythological.

Southey, Preface to *The Curse of Kehama*

Chapter Two:

Washington Irving and Muslim Spain

Washington Irving was already a well established traveler when he became an attaché of the USA to Madrid (1826-1829), and then Ambassador to the same capital in 1842. Living for a short while in Madrid at the house of the bibliographer, Obadiah Rich, owner of an extensive library of Spanish historical documents, he engaged himself in research for his popular *Chronicle of the Conquest of Granada* (1829). This work was followed by *The Alhambra* (1832), recalling fanciful legends of Moorish Spain, and by the conventional but unreliable biography of *Mahomet and His Successors* (1849-1850).[1] But the young Irving had already used Muslim materials in his contributions to *Salmagundi* (1807-1808),[2] long before he focused his romantic energies on the Islamic-Oriental world of Spain in his middle years.

The *Salmagundi* papers, serial essays with subject matter ranging from public morality, to manners, to social criticism, to humour, contain a series of fictitious letters by a foreign traveler par excellence, Mustapha Rub-a-Dub Keli Khan, a Tripolitan prisoner of the United States in the Barbary War, who was on parole in New York. Mustapha presents a point of view which is so alien to the society which he is observing that his reports of the most ordinary occurrences in New York make them out to be largely nonsensical. Mustapha's observation that American democracy has actually led to the creation of a logocracy of public hubris is a critique of the American political institutions. But Mustapha is immediately mystified by American customs to the degree that he can only be viewed as ignorant, if not silly. For example, he mistakes a Fourth of July celebration on the Battery for a pitched battle. Mustapha's conception of the American political system as a logocracy obviously has satirical associations, but his persistently mistaken observations about the simplest events are not only· funny, but also ridiculing, in that he himself turns out to be ridiculous in his observations. While Mustapha describes the American system of government as a logocracy, or "government of words" (p. 143), he comments satirically in Number Five on the Battery, "defended with formidable wooden bulwarks, which in the course of a hard winter were *thriftily* pulled to pieces by an *economic* corporation, to be distributed for fire-wood among the poor; this was done at the hint of a cunning old engineer, who assured them it was the only way in which their fortifications would ever be able to keep a *warm fire*" (p. 117). And our attention, as the papers advance, shifts to the fictional letter writer himself--to Mustapha's faith, harem, and native land. Writing home to Asem Hacchem, principal slave-driver, Rub-A-Dub Keli Khan remarks: "What then must be the feelings of thy unhappy kinsman, while thus lingering at an immeasurable distance from three-and-twenty of the most lovely and obedient wives in all Tripoli! Oh Allah! Shall thy servant never again return to his native land, nor behold his beloved wives, who beam on his memory beautiful as the rosy morn of the east, and graceful as Mahomet's camel!" (p. 91). Doomed to his captivity, Mustapha, by way of studying the alien society in which he is placed, comments extensively on the manners and customs of the "infidel" people he encounters. To his surprise, New York is so different and exotic that we laugh with Mustapha as much as we laugh at him. In comparing his native land to the most "magnificent city of the United States of America" (p. 90), Mustapha has but little to say, and what he says is often, as many passages reveal, a caricature. When he comments on the manner with which Americans conduct their elections, Mustapha, for example, tells his friend, Asem, that back home he lives "in a country where the people, instead of being at the mercy of a tyrant with a *million of heads*, have nothing to do but to submit to the will of a bashaw of only *three tails*" (p. 236). Whether a three-tailed Bashaw, or a million-headed governor such as they have in America is better, such a description goes beyond the verge of the absurd, as it is intended to do.

Eventually disgusted with "the vices and absurdities" (p. 283) of the strange society in which he is doomed to live, Mustapha finds but one thing to please him--women. Mustapha's *desire* becomes much more intense, being "an admirer of the sex" (p. 284), as he describes the world of amusement and playfulness women can afford. But Mustapha assures Asem, and perhaps his own disturbed self, that nothing "can shake from my heart the memory of former attachments" (p. 285). He adds "I listen with tranquil heart to the strumming and prattling of these fair syrens--their whimsical paintings touch not the tender chord of my affections; and I would still defy their fascinations, though they trailed after them trains as long as the gorgeous trappings which are dragged at the heels of the holy camel of Mecca [!]: or as the tail of the great beast in our prophet's vision, which measured three hundred and forty-nine leagues, two miles, three furlongs, and a hand's breadth in longitude" (p. 285). Mustapha extends his criticism of the socio-political, religious life which he has been observing to legends that had grown up around the Prophet, thus mixing the secular with the religious. So self-justification, in a way, becomes auto-accusation. Mustapha unintentionally ridicules the

Islamic tradition: he swears, for example, by the head, or beard, or camel of the Prophet. Certainly no such tradition exists in the Islamic lore. Mustapha also pokes fun at himself and his own country; he compares an election to "the Feast of Ramazan" (p. 190) and to other Muslim festivals and rituals. Mustapha's stupidity and narrow-mindedness are revealed in such recurrent words as the "sage" (pp. 310, 314), the "philosophical," and the "illustrious" (p. 90).[3] These Mustapha papers, however, are written at an early stage in Irving's literary career, and he left this subject matter and soon established himself as a popular romancer before returning to Muslim material more seriously.

Out of his study and observation in the Peninsula, Irving constructed material for such works as *The Conquest of Granada* (1829) and *The Alhambra* (1832).[4] Stanley Williams describes these successful, popular works this way:

> It was to be expected that in his histories Irving would show ... power in narrative and sensitivity to imagined scenes and emotions of Spanish past. The [story] of ... Boabdil's farewell to Granada is well told, and we share with Irving his fanciful re-creation of ... Boabdil's sorrow at his last [sight] of Granada. Though repetitious, the story never halt[s]. On and on [it] flow[s] with an enchanting ease, postponing from chapter to chapter the challenges of scholarship or the knotty questions of doctrine, belief, or institutional development. Indeed, the philosophical elements of history are always blandly absent. Perhaps it is difficult today to respect [such a book] as authentic history. Like *The Alhambra,* these chronicles of Christian knight and Moorish castle ... resemble glamorous, rather intricate fairy tales of ancient Spain. Irving's achievement was, in the end, a brilliant but dilettantish interpretation of priceless materials. He was the "discoverer," as one historiographer calls him, "of the fascination of Spain."[5]

That Washington Irving was fascinated with the mystery and romantic attractiveness of Moorish Spain is an acknowledged fact. And he in effect was the first American "discoverer" of the Peninsula. But *Granada* and *The Alhambra* both were fictionized history with little alloy of truth and much romance.

In a letter to Antoinette Bolviller, dated March 15, 1828, the year when he was presumably working on *The Conquest of Granada,* Irving speaks of his romantic fascination of Muslim Spain thus:

But Granada, bellissima Granada! Think what must have been over delight, when, after passing the famous bridge of Pinos, the scene of many a bloody encounter between Moor and Christian, and remarkable for having been the place where Columbus was overtaken by the messenger of Isabella, when about to abandon Spain in despair, we turned a promontory of the arid mountains of Elvira, and Granada, with its towers, its Alhambra, and its snowy mountains, burst upon our sight. The evening sun shone gloriously upon its red towers as we approached it, and gave a mellow tone to the rich scenery of the vega. It was like the magic glow which poetry and romance have shed over this enchanting place.[6]

Such an intoxicated imagination working on the picturesque past of the Moorish civilization and culture, with its poetic scenery, might have led Irving to write with some degree of haste, but with much fantasy, mingling the romantic with historical details.

Irving intended to do with his two-volume *Chronicle*, as he had already done with his earlier *History of New York* (1809-1812). But Fray Antonio Agapida is no Diedrich Knickerbocker. He is a prototype of the Spanish Catholic historian who can never see beyond the boundaries of his faith. Despite Irving's feelings for the Moors and for their heroism in their hopeless struggle to retain Granada, Agapida's religious bias always obtrudes. Early in the *Chronicle* Agapida reminds us that he would "relate the events of the conquest of Granada, where Christian knight and turbaned infidel disputed, inch by inch, the fair land of Andalusia, until the Crescent, that symbol of heathenish abomination, was cast down, and the blessed Cross, the tree of our redemption, erected in its stead."[7]

Agapida, Irving's chronicler, makes clear at the very outset that the Moors "fought for property, for liberty, for life," whereas the Christians "fought for glory, for revenge, for the holy faith, and for the spoil of these wealthy infidels" (p. 29). Interwoven with the authentic account of the conquest is Agapida's account of the history of Muslim Spain. At the time the *Chronicle* opens, Muley Aben Hassan is King of Granada, and has refused to pay the usual tribute to Ferdinand and Isabela, though his throne is none too stable. Aben Hassan's son, Boabdil el Chico, is dominated by a wife who has complete ascendency over the husband, and much ambition for her sons. However, after the Moors' defeat by the Christians at Alhama, Boabdil is elevated to the Crown as a king, eventually to surrender himself captive to the Christians. "The Christian historians of the time," Agapida tell us, "are sorely perplexed ... why so many Christian knights,

46

fighting in the cause of the holy faith, should thus miraculously, as it were, be given captive to a handful of infidel boors" (p. 78). So several bloody encounters between the Moors and the Christians, characterized by hatred and much mistrust, finally led to Boabdil's, and many others', pathetic departure from Granada. Nor was this the ultimate outcome of this warfare the object of which, observes Agapida, was "not the subjection of the Moors, but their utter expulsion from the land; so that there might no longer remain a single stain of Mahometanism throughout Christian Spain" (p. 103). Biased as it may be, Agapida's view here suggests little more than hostility. Many a bloody affair between Moors and Christians did take place, the result of which, after years of deadly struggle, was the end of the long Muslim rule in Spain. Agapida's monkish zeal prevents him from drawing a fair estimate of the Moors whom, towards the end of the *Chronicle*, when Granada is finally captured by the Christians, he still views as infidels whose "mosques and minarets should be converted into churches, and goodly priests and bishops should succeed to [their] alfaquis" (p. 391).

Despite this zealot for commentator, Irving's own feelings about the romance of the Moorish culture also comes out in the book as a kind of counterpoint. And Stanley Williams perceptively suggests that Irving's imaginative powers are at their best when, in his account of Boabdil el Chico's farewell to Granada, at the end of the Chronicle, the fair-haired monarch holds a sure place as a hero of romance in American fiction.[8] Nothing is more romantic than the scene when the Moors gather "to take a farewell gaze at their beloved city.... [They] gazed with a silent agony of tenderness and grief upon ... the scene of their loves and pleasures. While they yet looked [they realized] that the city was taken possession of, and the throne of the Moslem Kings was lost forever. The heart of Boabdil, softened by misfortunes and overcharged with grief, could no longer contain itself: 'Allah Achbar! God is great!' said he: but the words of resignation died upon his lips, and he burst into a flood of tears" (p. 415).

Writing to Colonel Aspinwall, his London agent for historical prose, Irving points out the degree to which he had adopted the picturings of the historical past as a literary metier:

> Literary excitement is excessively precarious, and there is
> nothing an author is made more readily distrustful of than the
> picturings of his fancy. We are mere chameleons, fed with
> air, and changing colour with everything with which we
> come in contact. We are to be stirred up to almost anything
> by encouragement and cheering, but the least whisper of

doubt casts a chill upon the feelings and the execution. *The Chronicle [of the Conquest of Granada]*, I am aware, is something of an experiment, and all experiments in literature or in any other thing are doubtful.... But I have made a work out of the old Chronicles, embellished as well as I am able, by the imagination, and adapted to the romantic taste of the day. Something that was to be between a history and a romance. Regarding Mr. Murray's suggestion that I ought to write him a light work in my old vein. I have some things sketched in a rough state in that vein, but thought it best to hold them back until I had written a work or two of more weight.[9]

Presumably what Irving had in mind were the legends and the sketches that later become *The Alhambra* (1832), having already experimented with the writing of romantic history, his coherent approach to the combination of fact and fiction that he wanted to create.

Since *The Alhambra* is designed as a Saracenic Salmagundi of exotic sketches, romantic fictions and folktales, and anecdotal essays, very much in the tradition as his earlier success, *The Sketch Book*, the book combines *Arabian Nights* material with factual description of the place and of the people Irving saw during the period of his residence there. Thus Irving makes travelogue an integral metaphor in *The Alhambra* and the exotic picturesque as an organizing form. The rural scenes, the foreign landscape, the poetic nature gradually emerge as an "admirable scene for a landscape painter."[10] Once Irving finishes with his romantic overview of Granada and the Alhambra, he immediately comes to sketches essentially about Moorish Spain's legends, history, and folktale. So the latter half of the book concerns itself with retelling narratives Irving has put in his own voice and style. The charm of "the Alhambraism"[11] Irving creates reflects the diversity of the Moorish, and thus Islamic, character of Spain.

But other than the fair-haired Boabdil of Granada, in *The Alhambra*, in addition to the romantic picturings of a dead past, we have an increasing concern about sexual matters (often, the Muslims, as will also be clear in *Mahomet*, are associated with sensual voluptuousness). "The legend of the Arabian Astrologer," for example, would at first sight seem to be as nothing more than a moral warning to the people in power against greed and excessive pride in maintaining their authority and power. In an case, the tale shows a concern with the effects of obsession with sensuality. Aben Habuz, a Moorish King, consults with an ancient Arabian astrologer to help him prevent marauders from threatening him and

48

taking his kingdom over. The aged astrologer, we are told, does invent a weathercock that points the direction of possible invasions, thus giving the king an actual advantage of using the magical instrument to maintain his rule. Yet the king is unmindful of his obligations to the astrologer once he is enamoured with a beautiful princess (p. 113). When the king rejects the counsellor's advice, the latter disappears with the beautiful princess into a magic garden, and the tale ends with the Moorish king once again besieged by foes. However, despite the moral didactic theme the story points out, Irving shows readiness to bring up the subject of sensuality and sexual matters when he, in his description of the palace of the Alhambra, early in the book, refers to "the voluptuous [Moorish] lords ... indulged in that dreamy repose so dear to the Orientalists" (p. 32). Other tales also suggest that Irving was prepared to deal with the received stereotype of the sensuality of the Moors.

Although in "The Legend of Prince Ahmed Al Kamel" Irving appears to have been trying to create a romance of adventure, the tale is an indirect satire on a young prince's sexual drive. Locked up in a seclusion by his father to keep him from sexual knowledge, the young prince eventually learns about love and beautiful women from a dove who plays the role of a go-between for the prince and a recluse princess. The prince finally manages to escape from his tower and goes in search of his young lady; but to win her hand he must overcome difficult obstacles. Two knowledgeable birds, the prince's advisors, are dubious about the value of love which the prince is in quest of. For, to them, to fall in love is not a happy prospect (pp. 138-143). Ignoring the birds' advice, the prince pursues his quest, though ignorant he may seem. He becomes deeply involved with conventional romantic notions. "'Is not love,' wonders he, 'the great mystery of nature, the secret principle of life ... of sympathy?'" (p. 141). But the parrot, with educated sarcasm perhaps, shouts "Where hast though learned this sentimental jargon?'" (p. 141). Preoccupied with his shallow romantic ideas, the prince has but little to say. And the counsellor birds show general indifference to his feelings, for they have their own worries.

> They traveled much more slowly than accorded with the impatience of the prince, but the parrot was accustomed to high life, and did not like to be disturbed early in the morning. The owl, on the other hand, was far sleeping at mid-day, and lost a great deal of time by his long siestas. His antiquarian taste was also in the way; for he insisted on pausing and inspecting every ruin, and had long legendary tales to tell about every old tower and castle in the country (p. 142).

The prince's innocence and untested simplicity do not suffice to gain him love. What he apparently lacks is the birds' competence. Left alone, then, Ahmed Al Kamel's chivalrous adventure to find his princess leads him to failure and despair instead.

Other references to love and sexual desire are in "The Legend of the Three Beautiful Princesses." When the Moorish king, Mohamed el Hayzari, is searching for a wife, for instance, he approaches a beautiful Spanish woman, who happens to be Christian, with a proposal of marriage. The damsel is repulsed by the aged king's ugliness, yet, in response, her duenna advises her to accept the king's proposal, even though he is an "infidel." The duenna asks the young woman

> "... What is there in all this to weep and wail about? Is it not
> better to be mistress of this beautiful palace, with all its gar-
> dens and fountains, than to be shut up within your father's old
> frontier tower? As to this Mohamed being an infidel what is
> that to the purpose? You marry him, not his religion; and if
> he is waxing a little old, the sooner you will be a widow, and
> mistress of yourself; at any rate, you are in his power, and
> you must either be a queen or a slave." (p. 177).

Doomed to her fate, the Spanish lady marries the king eventually, thus conver-ting, though only in appearance, to the faith of the royal husband. As the tale progresses, the king becomes a proud and happy father of three lovely princesses whom, following his counsellers' advice, he locks up in a tower so that he would be able to prevent them from learning about love. Kadiga, the duenna who wat-ches over the princesses to keep them from encountering young men, sends their father a message, as the princesses approach matrimonial age. She also sends

> ... a delicate little basket decorated with flowers, within
> which, on a couch of vine and fig-leaves, lay a peach, an
> apricot, and a nectarine, with their bloom and down and
> dewy sweetness upon them, and all in the stage of tempting
> ripeness. (p. 180).

When in the end the king's daughters meet, and flee with, potential Christian husbands, Irving reverses the situation of the father's marriage, suggesting that the women, like their father, have desires strong enough to make them arrange for a match. But Irving condemns the youngest sister to frustration and despair, even to an early death, for failure to pursue her passions by eloping with her own lover.

50

Although the sexual references we encounter in *The Alhambra* are far from daring, they show a kind of romantic voluptuousness in Moorish associations that captured Irving's imagination. Irving speaks of the delights he found in the Alhambra thus: "I inhale the odor of the rose, and feel the influence of the balmy climate, I am almost tempted to fancy myself in the paradise of Mahomet, and the plump little Dolores is one of the bright-eyed houris, destined to administer to the happiness of true believers" (p. 39). Obviously this is a reference to a sensual paradise which the Muslims, in Irving 's view, are supposed to have.

Writing to Henry Brevoort, when he left the Alhambra in 1829, Irving remarks that "never shall I meet on earth with an abode so much to my taste [the taste of an Orientalist perhaps], or so suited to my habits and pursuits."[12] Almost a month earlier he had written to Peter Irving pointing out how the Alhambra had infected his imagination:

> I had intended, however, to quit this place before long, and, indeed, was almost reproaching myself for protracting my sojourn, having little better than sheer self-indulgence to plead for it: for the effect of the climate, the air, the serenity, and sweetness of the place is almost as seductive as that of the castle of Indolence, and I feel at times the impossibility of working, or of doing anything but yielding to a mere voluptuousness of sensation. I found, therefore, that, like the Knight of Industry, it was necessary to break the charm and escape.[13]

It is this sense of sensuous voluptuousness which Irving wanted not only to capture, but also to develop as a theme throughout *The Alhambra*.[14]

Meanwhile, Irving's interest in Islamic history and culture reached its culmination, as Williams observes, in the two-volume *Mahomet and His Successors* (1849-1850).[15] Irving's immensely popular introduction of such romantic material as *The Conquest of Granada* and *The Alhambra*, which had begun in Rich's library, in turn originated an initial helter-skelter biographical and historical treatment of "The Lengendary Life of Mahomet,"[16] his first tentative notes toward what was to become *Mahomet and His Successors*.[17] Once more Irving availed himself of a stream of popular interest. The first volume concentrates on Muhammad's life, character, and person, but it also traces the rise and development of Islam through the character of the Prophet himself, giving interpretation of both Muhammad's character and the faith he proclaimed. The second volume proceeds with a rather simplistic interpretation of the lives of the companions of the Prophet and of the character of the Muslim Caliphate. I will devote more attention to the first volume; for the second volume contains only haphazard generalizations about the early Islamic history, which do not serve my concern here.

It may be assumed that Irving heavily relied on a number of contemporary sources that were inaccurate, unauthentic, and shallow. Though he made no explicit reference to it, Irving probably read Thomas Carlyle's lecture on "The Hero as Prophet. Mahomet: Islam", published in 1841. A new edition of Simon Ockley's *History of the Saracens* appeared in London in 1847. Also he was familiar with Gustav Weil's *Mohammed der Prophet* (1844) and apparently a number of similar sources like Marigny's *History of the Arabians* (1758), Gibbon's *Decline and Fall of the Roman Empire* (1776-1788), Ganginer's *Vie de Mahomet* (1748), Niebuhr's *Travels Through Arabia* (1792), Humphry Prideaux's *The True Nature of Imposture Fully Displayed in the Life of Mahomet* (1697), Samuel Green's *The Life of Mahomet* (1840), and George Sale's renowned translation of the Qur'an, first published in 1734.[18] With material from these sources Irving could not escape many of the current prejudices against Islam. For, to these authors, Muhammad is neither a Prophet, nor is he worthy of pro-phethood. It is not my purpose, however, to speculate about other, possibly more accurate, sources that Irving might have looked into, but it is germane to my purpose to show that Irving misrepresented Islam and the Prophet.

Irving, in his turn, adopted many of the long accepted views of Islam among the Christian polemicists; but he refabricated and reclothed some. Ockley's *History of the Saracens*, a copy of which Irving owned, was received at the time as "the most complete and authentic account of the Arabian Prophet and his successors" that exhibits "accuracy, judgment, taste, and scholarship."[19] Ockley's work is, of course, typical of an ongoing biased controversy against Islam, a controversy which repeats the common allegation that Muhammad is an impostor, and his religion is false.[20] Ockley's account of the Prophet's ascension into the Heavens Irving adopts, adding much romance and fancy to little alloy of truth,[21] in much the same way as he adopts Humphrey Prideaux's "vulgar manner" of writing the Prophet's name.[22]

Irving, in addition, asserts the view that Muhammad suffered from epileptic fits (pp. 33, 116), and he explains the change of *qiblah* (direction toward which the Muslims turn when in prayer) from Jerusalem to Makkah as a reaction to the Jews of Madinah, disregarding the fact that such a change had already taken place in Makkah long before Muhammad's flight to Madinah (p. 83). That Muhammad's religion was "one of violence and the sword" is also accepted by Irving.

52

"The sword," added he [the Prophet], "is the key of heaven
and hell, all who draw it in the cause of faith will be rewar-
ded with temporal advantages, every drop shed of their
blood, every peril and hardship endured by them, will be
registered on high as more meritorious than even fasting or
praying. If they fall in battle, their sins will at once be blotted
out, and they will be transported to paradise, there to reveal
in eternal pleasures in the arms of black-eyed houris." . . . .
Such were the doctrines and revelations which converted
Islamism of sudden from a religion of meekness and philan-
thropy to one of violence and the sword (p. 88).

While it did not spread by the sword, as Irving would suggest here, Islam did
teach that fighting in the cause of faith is worthwhile. And for the Prophet to have
believed that violence can be an instrument of faith, with which the religion was
to advance, is a hasty judgment. I do not intend here to say that the Muslims did
not use the sword in their battle against foes; they used it, but not for the sake of
mere violence. (The allegation that the Prophet spread his religion by the sword
ignored the fact that, at least during the early period, all of those who embraced
Islam did so through the proclaiming of the Qur'anic message.) Irving, however,
demonstrates that the Prophet's earliest enthusiasm had been corrupted by worldly
ambition, which in its turn led to the debasement of Islam itself:

He now arrived at the point where he completely diverged
from the celestial spirit of the Christian doctrines, and stam-
ped his religion with the alloy of fallible mortality. His
human nature was not capable of maintaining the sublime
forbearance he had hitherto inculcated . . . . He had come to
Medina a fugitive seeking an asylum, and craving merely a
quiet home. In a little while, and probably to his own surprise, he found an army at his command: for among the many
converts daily made in Medina, --the fugitives flocking to
him from Mecca, and proselytes from the tribes of the desert,
-- were men of resolute spirit, skilled in the use of arms, and
fond of partisan warfare. Human passions and mortal resent-
ments were awakened by this sudden access of power. They
mingled with that zeal for religious reform, which was still
his predominant motive. In the exaltations of his enthusiastic
spirit, he endeavored to persuade himself, and perhaps did so
effectually, that the power thus placed within his reach was a

means of effecting his great purpose, and that he was called upon by divine command to use it (p. 87).

Irving develops this simplistic interpretation of Islam as a perverted religion of the sword through the rest of *Mahomet and His Successors* and shows that "The moment [the Prophet] proclaimed the religion of the sword ... he was launched in a career of conquest, which carried him forward with its own irresistible impetus" (p. 198). Thus Muhammad, in Irving's view, becomes torn between his mission as a Prophet and his worldly interests and passions; thus Islam was characterized by bloodshed, and thus the Prophet compromised his religious mission with "that worldly alloy which at times was debasing his spirit, now that he had become the Apostle of the Sword." (p. 123)

Connected with the sword is a sensual paradise. Irving's conception of paradise is extremely romantic. For, while it is true that the faithful will receive rewards for their good deeds, and that they may be admitted to an ever-lasting paradise, Irving was temperamentally predisposed to agree with the received allegation that the Muslim paradise was a landscape replete with every voluptuous convenience and with black-eyed houris to satisfy the lustful Muslims. Here is a revealing view of Irving's conception of the sensual delights the faithful will enjoy in paradise:

> Above all, the faithful will be blessed with female society to the full extent even of Oriental imagings. Besides the wives he had on earth, who will rejoin him in all their pristine charms, he will be attended by the Hur al Oyun, or Houris, so called from their large black-eyes; resplendent beings, free from every human defect or fraility; perpetually retaining their youth and beauty, and renewing their virginity. Seventy-two of these are allotted to every believer. The intercourse with them will be fruitful or not according to their wish, and the offspring will grow within an hour to the same stature with the parents (p. 211).[23]

From the viewpoint of the Christian polemicists, paradise (often Muhammad's paradise, Muhammad's houris, Muhammad's delights) is that of sexual (but not spiritual) gratification. This was one of the points of criticism directed against Islam, or rather "Mahometism," the religion of the polygamous Prophet who could never think of paradise except in terms of sexual laxity, and whose religion dictates that the Muslims fight the infidels by promising them black-eyed houris

54

in the next world. Anticipating the Prophet's paradise, therefore, can also indicate enjoying earthly houris (numerous wives), who would be willing to gratify, like their faithful counterparts.

Suffice it to say, therefore, that Irving was caught unwittingly in an ongoing dialogue against Islam. Irving's information came through muddy channels, and he seems to have been overwhelmed by the sources he read so much that he confused events and facts. For example, he suggests, early in the biography, that the Prophet's mother was Jewish (p. 40). This is certainly false, for the Prophet's mother was a Qurashite who followed her tribe's beliefs and their respect for the Ka'abah. Later in the biography, Irving also tells us of the Qurayshi messengers to the Najashi, the Abyssinian king, to obtain the Muslim fugitives while the Prophet is in Madinah in the second year of his flight, the *Hijrah* (p. 100). This event actually took place in the fifth year of Muhammad's mission, almost seven years before he left for Madinah. With errors of fact such as these,[24] one can argue that Irving's work is neither reliable, nor accurate. For when he constructed material for his biography of Muhammad, he did not, of course, question the accuracy and reliability of his sources, reiterating thus the same traditional misconceptions of Islam and the Prophet. Irving did, however, endeavour to introduce enough facts into his biography to make it an interesting work for the common reader, a work which, he hoped, would even lead to a better conception of Islam and the Muslims. But his overall concern was with romantic history and not with the accuracy of information. So he borrowed freely from a wide range of sources to produce a *romantic* work which would entertain, and simultaneously enlighten, an unquestioning audience. His entire work is a generally appealing mixture of fact and fiction directed towards the reading public.

Muhammad can also be seen as lustful. Out of much romance and less care for the historical fact, perhaps, Irving depicts the person of the Prophet thus:

> In some respects he was a voluptuary. "There are two things in this world," would he say, "which delight me, women and perfumes. These two things rejoice my eyes, and render me more fervent in devotion." From his extreme cleanliness, and the use of perfumes and of sweet-scented oil for his hair, probably arose that sweetness and fragrance of person, which his disciples considered innate and miraculous. His passion for the sex had an influence over all his affairs. It is said that when in presence of a beautiful female, he was continually smoothing his brow and adjusting his hair, as if anxious to appear to advantage (p. 193).

The entire picture of the Prophet here is in some ways marred by exaggeration and by the selection of preconceived details. The sexual language used above suggests, but the syntax never states this, that Muhammad can do nothing but gratify and copulate, since his "passion for the sex had an influence over all his affairs." Indeed the Prophet encouraged cleanliness not because he was "in some respects a voluptuary," but because he wanted it to be part of every Muslim's faith.

The Prophet's sensuality is stressed further when Irving allows him to fall in love with the physical charms of his adopted son's wife, Zeinab, so that she may become his own wife. Irving tells us:

> One day [the Prophet] entered [Zeid's] house with the free-
> dom with which a father enters the dwelling of a son. Zeid
> was absent, but Zeinab, his wife, whom he had recently mar-
> ried, was at home. She was the daughter of Djasch, of the
> country of Kaiba, and considered fairest of her tribe. In the
> privacy of home she had laid aside her veil and part of her
> attire, so that her beauty stood revealed to the gaze of
> Mahomet on his sudden entrance. He could not refrain from
> expressions of wonder and admiration, to which she made no
> reply, but repeated them all to her husband on his return.
> Zeid knew the amorous susceptibility of Mahomet, and saw
> that he had been captivated by the beauty of Zeinab.
> Hastening after him he offered to repudiate his wife; but the
> prophet forbade it as contrary to the law. The zeal of Zeid
> was not to be checked; he loved his beautiful wife, but he
> venerated the Prophet, and he divorced himself without
> delay. when the requisite term of separation had elapsed,
> Mahomet accepted, with gratitude, this pious sacrifice. His
> nuptials with Zeinab surpassed in splendor all his other mar-
> riages. His doors were thrown open to all comers; they were
> feasted with the flesh of sheep and lambs, with cakes of bar-
> ley, with honey, and fruits, and favorite beverages; so they
> ate and drank their fill and then departed -- railing against the
> divorce as shameful and the marriage as incestuous (p. 112).

The story of Zeid's wife (Zeid, the Prophet's freedman) had been a favourite thesis against the veracity of Muhammad's claim to prophethood since the Middle Ages. The story does have a basis in fact. The relevant facts, which no Muslim,

Muhammad himself included, has attempted to suppress, or cast doubt upon, are simply as follows. Visiting Zeid's house, Muhammad was met at the door by Zeid's wife, Zeinab, who was indeed wearing a light garment, which the Arab women used to wear in the privacy of the house at the time. Her husband was not at home, so Muhammad immediately withdrew muttering praise to Allah. Zeinab was an attractive woman and Muhammad could see that she was, for, after all, she had been brought up under his care, and it was he who asked her hand for Zeid. Zeid divorced Zeinab. Having been divorced, there was a crucial problem for Muhammad to marry her. Zeid, we realize, was the Prophet's adopted son, and it was the custom among the Arabs at the time to treat adopted sons like one's own sons. And according to that tradition Muhammad could not consider marrying Zeinab even if he desired to. It was revealed to him at this critical point that he should follow the ways of Allah and not his nation's customs. Thus it was Allah's decree that Muhammad may marry divorced Zeinab if he wanted to (which in fact Muhammad did.) But his marriage was to set a precedent to the Muslims that to marry a divorced adopted son's wife is neither sinful, nor socially unacceptable.[25]

Towards the end of the first volume of the biography, while he discusses the question of Muhammad's imposture, Irving asserts that the "general tenor of the Prophet's conduct up to the time of his flight from Mecca, is that of an enthusiast acting under a species of mental delusion, deeply involved with a conviction of his being a divine agent for religious reform ..., which he sought to substitute for the blind idolatry of his childhood" (p. 196-197). The "mental delusion" that Irving mentions here is somewhat different and softened from earlier allegations of imposture. His final verdict on Muhammad is: sincere but deluded. There is nothing new in ideas like epilepsy, love, and desire; all had been alleged before. Nevertheless, the new perspective from which these conventionalized themes were seen is imbued with a newly awakened romantic interest that was reflected in Irving's historical study of Muhammad and Islam. Being a better romantic writer than those who wrote about the Prophet before him, Irving excelled in popularizing his treatment of Muhammad and his successors. His romantic method no doubt added to the fascination of this experiment particularly because he put in it so much of popular interpretations, predictable vocabulary, fantasy, and, sometimes, remoteness from reality. Indeed romantic but unauthentic is Irving's treatment of the Prophet.

Irving claims neither "novelty of fact, nor profoundity of research," but he asserts that he wanted to present "admitted facts" concerning Muhammad's life (p. 3). And he tried hard to reflect an image of a serious, fact-conscious historian who wanted to present a detailed analysis of the Prophet's life. As a romancer,

Irving was somewhat constrained by "facts" and challenged by them to unleash his imaginative skills with exotic details which would appeal more to him as a story teller, and to the reader's feelings and imagination than to the historian's precision. As Stanley Williams rightly observes, "in no book of Irving's is there so weary a distaste for control of source material," as in *Mahomet*, "or for those other principles which he had followed rigorously in some of his other historical writings. He avoided discussion of conflicting evidence; he almost entirely omitted documentation; in many parts of this book he even dispensed with his beloved process of 'toning,' admitting that he offered merely a digest of the originals. These reappear, accordingly, as lifeless . . . . "[26] Irving's negligence of documentation was most probably due to the fact that he was pressured for time because of his obligation to the publisher for the Author's Revised Edition. Perhaps, as E.N. Feltskog suggests, Irving's "Failures of organization and assimilation of his materials ... seem the result of haste and even a downright unfamiliarity with his sources .... Irving was trying to keep up with Putnam's demands for new copy for the Author's Revised Edition, and the confusions of narrative, his obvious errors of fact and interpretation, and his outright plagiarisms from Marigny and Ockley show that [*Mahomet and His Successors*] was finally a listless piece of literary hack work."[27] Nevertheless, Irving's own taste was directed more towards the romantic than factual accuracy.

In his use of source material, Irving tended to adopt certain events that could best serve the imagination of a litterateur, but hardly that of a historian. For, as a historian, Irving did not seem to have cared for accuracy much, he was even at liberty to present dramatized dialogues, as it were, that suited his romantic taste.[28] After all, Irving did not place much reliance on scholarly research, as Williams reminds us here and there in his critical assessment of Irving, but, on the other hand, Irving excelled in the world of anecdote and romance. Had he approached *Mahomet* with an objective concern for historical truthfulness, his endeavour could have definitely been a much more reliable source. But inaccurate as it is, Irving's work holds a sure place among his romantic conceptions of Moorish, and thus Islamic, history and character.

Irving's interest in the Prophet in turn led to further popular but lesser known literature such as *Mohammed, The Arabian Prophet* (1850) by George Henry Miles, a lawyer and teacher in Baltimore.[29] This tragedy was written in competition for a prize of one thousand dollars offered by the actor Edwin Forrest, and Miles won the prize over a hundred competitors with his five-act tragedy. Forrest did not use the play, but it was performed in 1851 at the Lyceum Theater in New York. In the play Muhammad is conceived of as a man who, believing himself a prophet, asserts his mission by imposture. While there is no explicit connection between Irving's *Mahomet* and Miles' tragedy, the latter remains typical of a common tradition that perpetuates false conceptions of Islam and the Prophet. While Irving had covered the details of the life of the Prophet from his infancy and childhood to his death and the attending circumstances thereof, the contemporary Miles restricts himself in scope. He looks at the life of the Prophet from the age of forty, when Muhammad received revelation to his death, a period of twenty years during which, Miles asserts, the Prophet "invented" the visions that granted him supernatural authority. That the Prophet is a "sincere impostor"[30] Miles undoubtedly accepts. Yet, he explains in the "Preface," it would be "no compliment to Christianity, to make Mohammed a monster; it is rather a bitter sneer at human credulity. The lesson conveyed by the life and death of the Arabian impostor, is the inability of the greatest man, starting with the purest motives, to counterfeit a mission from God, without becoming the slave of hell" (pp. vii-viii). In effect, Miles does not make a "monster", but a counterfeit of Muhammad as a prophet of God, and thus he turns out to be neither a prophet, nor worthy of prophethood!

From the very outset, Miles finds nothing in Muhammad's person but sensuality, ambition, and imposture. But if Miles believed Muhammad to be an impostor, what kind of hero was he likely to make out of him in his tragedy? Obviously, it is awkard to portray a hero as a mere villainous deceiver, for, judging from the Preface, Muhammad's character and religion were to be presented as a blend of "truth and falsehood, sincerity and deceit" (p. vi), and this split-vision approach follows the outlines of the Prophet's life as far as it was known to Miles. We have no way of knowing what source material Miles consulted,[31] but we do know that his tragedy involves the representation of the Prophet as an enthusiast whose mission was of some value to the "idolatrous" Arabs! It appears also that Miles wanted to represent Muhammad as a sensualist who could easily fall for the machinations of women. The sexual gratification of Muhammad, almost to the total dismissal of the spiritual purity of a Prophet, becomes more or less a mere eroticism. This is how, for example, Miles displays the Prophet's sensuality:

> Moh. Leap, my glad heart! [addressing his wife,
>   Khadijah] Sweet mistress of my soul,
> Thy head, unpillowed and erect again,
> Shall droop no more till -- (*He kisses her.*)
> Hell! -- thy lips are fire.
> In Allah's name what lured thee from thy bed?

Hot as Orion, in thy thrilling veins
The fever flames --Return! (p. 39)

The Prophet here is able to suppress neither a curse, nor desire. But he is evidently capable of being tender in love, given the right kind of woman.

Following Khadijah's death, the Prophet marries Ayshah, the daughter of his intimate companion, Abu Bakr. What is interesting here, in addition to the exhausted theme of voluptuousness, is an agonizing love intrigue between Ayshah and the Prophet's cousin, Ali, that Miles makes up. Irritated, as the Prophet could be, this is the kind dialogue we have between the Prophet and his wife:

Moh. This to thy Prophet?
    Ayes. Yes! When man discards
The peal of chastity, he cannot ask
His wife to treasure it. Ay, make the earth
As full of houris as thy Paradise!
Free all thy slaves, and marry all their wives!
Indulge thy lust --
    Moh. 'Tis my prerogative.
A Prophet's not a woman, doomed to freeze
In chaste fidelity to one poor mortal.
Away! -- (*She is going -- he stops her.*)
And yet, -- if not in thee, Ayesha,
Where shall I soothe my agony?
    Ayes. In God. (p. 125)[32]

The sensual element that the dialogue contains needs not much commentary, for it had been the accepted norm. Muhammad here all but supersedes Allah in His function: he not only commands those attractive spiritual beings, the houris, but he also has a paradise (paradise is always Muhammad's not Allah's.) It is Muhammad who is irritated and he who should be appeased. All this makes it abundantly clear to contemporary readers that a man who behaved in this way, especially with women, could not possibly be a prophet at all!

Presumably the need to "defend" Christianity led Miles to accept on face value many of the points which fitted in with his preconceived notions, to communicate to the reading public "facts" which gave a "favourable" view of Muhammad. Miles, perpetuating a common tradition, assumed that Muhammad was dishonest and he made this assumption the basis of his tragedy. In the play, therefore, it was not uneasy to go on to hold that Muhammad was a fanatical leader who had schemed himself into power by claiming to have received revelations, and that he in addition was a victim of the irreconcilable conflict between his mission as inspired Prophet and the exigencies of his temporal sway over all Arabia; thus Islam was the religion of the sword, and thus Muhammad was a Prophet.

> Moh. Hail crescent moon! 'tis Allah's
>   finger brands
> Thy flaming curve upon the sapphire sky,
> A beacon and a symbol to his Prophet!
> Hail, scimitar of vengeance! not in vain
> The token flames. Hence forth, Mohammed, drop
> The servile imitator, and amaze
> Mankind--a witness to the power of God, --
> The Prophet of the Sword! (p. 82)[33]

It was by the sword; by violence and terror, then, that Muhammad became "a witness to the power of God," and that Islam, as a developed religion, began by the sword and was maintained by the sword. But for the Prophet to have believed that the sword can be used as an instrument of faith, as it were, with which the religion of the Prophet was to advance is a little absurd!

Muhammad was then supposed in the play to have availed himself of this instrument of faith (the sword) to gain lordship over the scattered tribes of Arabia, and to obtain the "crown" of prophethood he always desired.

> Moh. But now, -- the man is lost within
>   the prophet,--
> The voice of Allah is my only will;
> Before his high command, all earthly ties
> Melt like the morning mist; and though his hand
> Crush my bruised heart with all its best affections,
> Still, with a harrowed breast and tear-worn cheek,
> I'll stagger through the wreck of human feeling,
> And, toiling upward, scale the mount of God--
> Fulfil my mission, and obtain my crown! (p. 28)[34]

Obviously, Miles seems to have been prepared to show that the "royal" Prophet was an enthusiast, but he also suggests that from enthusiasm to fanaticism to

61

imposture the steps were slippery and that Muhammad made the ascent simply in being "lost within the Prophet." Ambition, he holds, was the chief motive in Muhammad's mission and nothing else.

> I'll scourage the world!
> Still in the prime and majesty of manhood,
> With all the appetites and edge of youth
> Unblunted, --I shall now begin to taste
> The joys a Prophet should. Plucked their
>   thrones.
> Bareheaded kings shall tremble at my feet,
> And queens adorn my bed. (p. 116).

Linked to the sword and worldly ambition is a heavenly paradise of sensuality and voluptuousness. Here is an example of Miles's presentation of the sensual delights that the Muslims will enjoy in Paradise:

> Moh: To all who die beneath this sacred standard
> I promise Eden's loftiest couches, lined
> With greenest silk, impregned with gold and gems.
> Around them flowering branches shall mature
> Embracing fruits, and twining roses shade
> Their perfumed limbs. Immortal houris-maids
> Fairer than any wanton fancy ever shaped,
> Whose large black eyes are virgin to their lords
> Whose cheeks dissolve the ruby in the pearl.   (p. 95).

Like Irving's, Miles's view of Muslim paradise is at this point purely in the romantic tradition. For, while it is true that the good among the Muslims may enjoy an ever-lasting paradise, Miles agreed with the received allegation that paradise was simply a heavenly place imbued with every voluptuous grace from God and with black-eyed maids (houris) to satisfy the lustful Muslims, a paradise of sexual (but not spiritual) gratification at best.

It should be necessary to labour the point that Muhammad's violence, self-indulgence, and dishonesty are palpable distortions: but further assessment and criticism will not be out of place. Miles did not succeed in portraying a coherent and convincing characterization of Muhammad; he was too unsympathetic to the man, his religion, and the culture it produced, to be able to treat him fairly and dispassionately. As we can see, the difference is slight between Miles' Muhammad and the "Mahounde" of the Middle Ages. It is clear that he was still unable to think of Islam as anything other than Muhammad and his sword. Such an unflattering image of Islam is obviously shallow and distorted. While it is not surprising that this distortion should have been formed during the medieval period, as I have shown in the previous chapter, there are some grounds for surprise in the fact that the distorted image has persisted in the Western literary tradition, but on narrower grounds. Miles' treatment of Muhammad represented the prevailing opinion: ambition achieved by way of imposture; and lust, exemplified by Muhammad's sanction of polygamy, and by his paradise of sensual delights.

However, during the first four decades of the nineteenth century a greater expansion of the literature dealing with the matter of the Muslim Orient emerged. The expansion was possibly due not only to the increased interest in the Muslim East stimulated by travel reports, but also to the search by writers participating in the romantic movement, who were encouraged by the demands of an enlarged appreciative public, for exotic subject matter taken from the culture, manners, and customs of the region. In the field of interpretation of the life Muhammad and of the history of Islam, with the exception of the unsuccessful endeavour of Irving, there was no new development of significance. Some of the older legends about Muhammad had disappeared. Muhammad's death brought on by drunkenness, his being devoured by swine, his epileptic fits were no longer reiterated. The bull bearing the Qur'an, the trained pigeon picking grain from the Prophet's ears, and the Prophet's coffin suspended at Makkah had also disappeared. But the reductionist view of the Prophet as impostor, remains popular, as exemplified in Miles' rather weak attempt at tragedy. Irving's work at least popularized the Moorish material for its possibilities as romance.

Notes

1 See Stanley T. Williams's *The Life of Washington Irving*, 2 vols. (1935; rpt. New York: Octagon Books, 1971), the authoritative work on Washington Irving.

2 The question as to whether Irving, or his collaborators initiated the episodes dealt with below remains unsettled, though Paulding seems to be the more likely candidate. Irving, however, wrote only portions of the Mustapha papers. See Bruce Granger and Martha Hartzog, "Assignments of Authorship," in *Oldstyle; Salmagundi* (Boston: Twayne Publishers, 1978), pp. 327-336. References in the text are to this edition.

3 See other passages on pp. 117, 123, 171, 195, 315.

4 The "Chronicle of the Ommiades" was also one of the narratives of the early Moorish history which Irving sketched out while in Spain in 1827, and revised twenty years later. The narrative was left unpublished at his death. Irving intended the Chronicle to summarize the reign of the Omayyades in Spain from 752 to 1030 A.D. See *Miscellaneous Writings*, 1803-1859, ed. Wayne R. Kime (Boston: Twayne Publishers, 1981), II, 202-232. This was preceded by *Abu Hassan*, a light opera, which Irving wrote in collaboration with the English playwright Barham J. Livius in 1823. The play, which is essentially an elaboration of a passage taken from the *Arabian Nights*, involves a certain Abu Hassan who has long been in debt to the Caliph's banker, Omar. The overbearing creditor decides not to wait any longer, making a demand on Abu Hassan for immediate payment. When he fails to meet the demand, Abu Hassan asks his wife, Fatima, to use her attractiveness to appease Omar's anger. Omar finally falls victim to Fatima's charms and offers his credit as a price for her favors. But the Caliph comes to know the story, ordering that Omar be dismissed out of court. See the whole play in *Miscellaneous Writings*, I, 192-227.

5 *The Spanish Background of American Literature*, I, 142. Williams sees *Granada* as "a curious blend of history and legend" (I, 142). See, however, Irving's own "Review of a *Chronicle of the Conquest of Granada*," in *Miscellaneous Writings*, II, 4-30. Irving wrote this review in an effort to dispel the doubts about the work as a historical narrative.

6 Washington Irving, *Letters, 1823-1838*, ed. Ralph M. Aderman, et al. (Boston: Twayne Publishers, 1979), II, 281-282; henceforth cited as *Letters*.

7 *A Chronicle of the Conquest of Granada* (New York: P.F. Voillier and Son, n.d.), p. 9. Other references in the text follow this edition.

8 *The Spanish Background of American Literature*, II, 42.

9 Ben H. McClary, ed., *Washington Irving and The House of Murry: Geoffrey Crayon Charms the British, 1817-1856* (Knoxville: University of Tennessee Press, 1969), p. 120.

10 Williams T. Lenhan and Andrew B. Myres, ed., *The Alhambra* (Boston: Twayne Publishers, 1983), p. 9. Subsequent references in the text refer to this edition.

11 Williams' term. See *The Spanish Background of American Literature*, II, 44.

12 *Letters*, II, 461.

13 *Letters*, II, 447.

14 Irving develops this sense of voluptuousness through the rest of *The Alhambra*. In the "Legend of the Moor's Legacy," for instance, Irving, while he condemns the wealthy aspirations of Senora Gil, a water-carrier's wife, shows that she "befringed, belaced, and betassled from her head to her heels, with glittering rings on every finger, became a model of slattern fashion and finery" (p. 173). After having once been a poor, pugnacious woman, Senora Gil became decorated with the finery and taste of an Oriental bride, if not a harlot, through her sudden elevation into aristocracy and wealth. See also "The Tower of Las Infantas," "The Legend of the Rose of the Alhambra," and the "Legend of the Two Discreet Status."

15 *The Life of Washington Irving*, II, 223.

16 Irving took notes on the life of Muhammad when in Madrid early in 1827, possibly in conjunction with his studies for *The Conquest of Granada* and *The Alhambra*. In 1831 he offered John Murray, his London Publisher, part of "The Legendary Life of Mahomet," in which Murray was not interested. Back in Spain as a diplomat, Irving read further about Muhammad, and finally, in 1849, published a complete volume suited for popular reading.

17 See "Historical Notes," in *Mahomet and His Successors*, ed. Henry A. Pochmann and E.N. Feltskog (Madison: University of Wisconsin Press, 1970), 522-23. Subsequent references in the text follow this edition.

18 *Ibid.*, 530-535. I actually have no substantial evidence that Irving followed closely these books, but Layla Abed al-Salam al-Farsy shows that he owed them a great deal. See "Washington Irving's *Mahomet*: A Study of the Sources", Diss. University of Wisconsin, Milwaukee, 1983.

19 Simon Ockley, *History of the Saracens*, 2 vols. (1718; rpt. London: George Bell and Sons, 1878), pp. i-ii. Ockley's book certainly was one of the sources Irving turned to; he misspelled, for instance, the name of the slave who killed the Prophet's uncle, Hamzah, as "Wacksa" (*Mahomet*, p. 107) instead of Washi, repeating thus Ockley's error (Ockley, p. 37).

20 *Ibid.*, pp. 63-71.

21 *Mahomet*, pp. 63-71; Ockley, pp. 20-30.

22 Prideaux, in T*he True Nature of Imposture* (London: E. Curll, 1723), chooses to use the common, popular form of the transliterated name (Mahomet), though he knows there is a more "accurate" one (Mohammed). See p. xvi.

23 See also pp. 210, 212.

24 Irving also commits other errors of fact. Commenting on the practice of fasting among the Muslims during the month of Ramadan, Irving declares that the devout believer is to abstain from "baths and perfumes." Actually the Muslims do abstain from eating and drinking, and from sexual gratification during the day, but for them not to take baths or use perfume is beyond belief (*Mahomet*, p. 215). He also tells us that, in addition to the regular five prayers every Muslim should perform, a sixth prayer may be volunteered "between the first watch of the night and the dawn of day" (p. 214). Voluntary prayer may be performed at any time, and it is not necessarily limited to a sixth prayer.

25 See for more detail Muhammad H. Haykal, *The Life of Muhammad*, trans. Ismail al-Faruqi (North American Trust Publications, 1976), pp. 294-297.

26 *Life of Washington Irving*, II, 224.

27 See "Historical Notes," in *Mahomet*, p. 546.

28 See, for example, the dialogue between Omar and his sister. *Mahomet*, pp. 50-51.

29 Information about Miles is scanty and widely scattered. See, however, *The Library of Southern Literature* (Atlanta: The Martin and Hoyt Co., 1909), viii, 3641-3662; and *The Dictionary of American Biography* (New York: Charles Scribner's Sons, 1933), xii, 611-612.

30 *Mohammed, The Arabian Prophet: A Tragedy in Five Acts* (Boston: Philips, Sampson and Company, 1850), p. vi. Other references from this edition are cited in the text.

31 There is a hint at pp. vi and 156 that Miles might have read, or at least have been familiar with, Voltaire's *La Fanatisme, Ou Mahomet* (1742), E.W.

Lane's *An Account of the Manners and Customs of the Modern Egyptians* (1836), Goethe's *Mahomet Gesang* (1773), Edward Gibbon's *The Decline and Fall of the Roman Empire* (1788), Prideaux's *The True Nature of Imposture* (1697), and Irving's *Mahomet*.

32 See also pp. 51, 88, 95, 126.

33 See also p. 98.

34 See also pp. 121, 153.

Life in the East is fierce, short, hazardous, and in extremes. Its elements are few and simple, not exhibiting the long range and undulation of European existence, but rapidly reaching the best and the worst.

          Emerson, "Persian Poetry"

Go, let us ask of Constantine
To loose his grasp on Poland's throat;
And beg the lord of Mahmoud's line
To spare the struggling Suliote;
Will not the scorching answer come
From turbaned Turk, and scornful Russ:
"Go, loose your fettered slaves at home,
then turn and ask the like of us!"

          Whittier, "Expostulation"

Chapter Three :

Emerson and Whittier: American Thought and
the Idea of the Orient

The romance of Washington Irving's Orientalism differs considerably from Ralph Waldo Emerson's and the transcendentalists' interest in the Orient. The involvement of Emerson, Thoreau, and Alcott in Oriental thought is essentially part of the beginnings of comparative religion as a field for study,[1] but it goes beyond that. In Emerson's case it influences his writing--particularly his interest in, and admiration for, the Sufi poets. In 1822, a year after his graduation from college, writing to his mentor and favorite aunt, Mary Moody Emerson, who informed him of Oriental books she had recently come upon, Emerson remarks:

> I am curious to read your Hindu mythologies. One is apt to
> lament over indolence and ignorance, when he reads some of
> those sanguine students of the Eastern antiquities, who seem
> to think that all the books of knowledge, and all the wisdom
> of Europe twice-told, lie hid in the treasures of the Bramins
> and the volumes of Zoroaster. When I lie dreaming on the
> possible contents of pages, as dark to me as the characters on
> the Seal of Solomon, I console myself with calling it lear-
> ning's El Dorado. Every man has a fairy land just beyond the
> compass of his horizon ... and it is very natural that literature
> at large should look for some fanciful stores of mind which
> surpassed example and possibility.[2]

It seems probable that Emerson had already known something of the Orientals long before he wrote this letter to his aunt, as Frederic I. Carpenter suggests.[3] But as yet he is not fully aware of them. The course of correspondence between Mary Moody Emerson and her nephew marked not only the presence of the Orient at the dawning of Emerson's intellectual development, but also his admiration for it. In turn Aunt Mary's enthusiasm led to and encouraged the youth's life-long habit of speaking of the Orient. A few months earlier Emerson had written:

I was the pampered child of the East. I was born where the
soft western gale breathed upon me fragrance of cinnamon
groves and through the seventy windows of my hall the eye
fell on the Arabian harvest. An hundred elephants, appareled
in cloth of gold, carried my train to war, and the smile of the
Great King beamed upon Omar. But now--the broad Indian
moon looks through the broken arches of my tower, and the
wing of desolation fans me with poisonous airs; the spider's
threads are the tapestry which adorns my walls and the rain
of night is heard in my halls for the music of the daughters of
Cashmere.[4]

At this stage Emerson's Orientalism, Arthur Christy suggests, was not yet
"disciplined by many books."[5] Though undisciplined it may be, the early phase of
Emerson's Orientalism shows an awareness of the outlandish and the inaccessible
--the other half of the world--an awareness of its attractiveness, romance, poetry,
and religion. Such an awareness of the Orient constitutes only fragments of
fantasy that reflect Emerson's preoccupation with exoticism. "The Arabian harvest" is at variance with Indian Cashmere, and is of course of a different taste,
and Omar, whether the second Muslim Caliph or not, is difficult to associate with
the beams of the Indian Moon. But Emerson did not linger much on these matters.
What concerned him is the romantic suggestiveness of the "cinnamon groves,"
"the broken arches," "the cloth of gold," and "the broad Indian Moon" as a
source of literary enchantment with the Orient. These early quotations show little
knowledge on Emerson's part of Oriental literatures and religions. As Frederic
Carpenter perceptively suggests, Emerson's immature interest in the Orient varied
between "fascination and aversion."[6] But the feeling of aversion predominated in
his early writing. For thirteen years, from the age of twenty-one to thirty-four, the
period from 1824 to 1837, Emerson did not record any significant ideas or concern with the Orient, either Islamic or non-Islamic. Perhaps this lack of interest
was due to the difficulty in obtaining sufficient information. Later in his career
Emerson exploited the attractive mystery of the Orient and appropriated much of
its culture to his own uses. But he was not an Orientalist himself, though he
gradually began to rediscover Oriental material and to read all the Islamic books
he came upon.[7]

There is no certain proof, observes Arthur Christy, as to when Emerson
practically came under the influence of Oriental thought.[8] But it is evident that
Greek Platonism was the chief element in formulating his Orientalism, which was
a relatively late development in Emerson's career. "The kernel of Emerson's

Orientalism"[9] to use Carpenter's words, lies in his series of Occidental biographical lectures, *Representative Men* (1850). Though it did not offer much space for specific Islamic material, the book contained references to it, especially in the essay on "Plato." The first sentence in the essay reads: "Among secular books, Plato only is entitled to Omar's fanatical compliment to the Koran, when he said, 'Burn the libraries; for their value is in this book.'"[10] The application of Omar's statement on the Qur'an (alleged to be said at the conquest of Alexandria) to Plato's work brings East to West whereby certain boundaries and categories are established, associations and distinctions created. The Orient is given a space where it stands vis-à-vis the Occident. While in Egypt "Plato ... imbibed the idea of one Deity," writes Emerson, "in which all things are absorbed." And thus "The unity of Asia, and the detail of Europe; the infinitude of the Asiatic soul and the defining, result-loving, machine-making, surface-seeking, opera-going Europe, -- Plato came to join, and, by contact, to enhance the energy of each. The excellence of Europe and Asia are in his brain. Metaphysics and natural philosophy expressed the genius of Europe; he substructs the religion of Asia, as the base" (*Works*, IV, 53-54). While Asia is associated with the soul and "religion", Europe is associated with the mind and "Metaphysics and natural philosophy". This distinction suppresses Asiatic religions to a substructural level. But their presence as "the base" of European culture is, though reductionist, of significance. Plato's arrival in ancient Egypt is an arrival of defining, and "This defining is philosophy" (*Works*, IV, 47). "At last, comes Plato," writes Emerson, "the distributor who needs no barbaric paint, or tattoo, or whooping; for he can define. He leaves with Asia the vast and superlative; he is the arrival of accuracy and intelligence" (*Works*, IV, 47). Form the very outset, Emerson initiates his analysis by distinguishing the "Two Cardinal facts" at the base of all human philosophy: what he considers as "the one, and the two," or Unity and Variety (*Works*, IV, 47). The split had appeared and reappeared in many forms: as the one and the many, being versus intellect, rest versus motion, and finally East versus West. The key passage follows: "The country of unity, of immovable institutions ... of men faithful in doctrine and in practice to the idea of a deaf, unimplorable, immense fate, is Asia .... On the other side, the genius of Europe is active and creative." East and West are intellectually defined here. The difference between them is neither geographical, nor racial. It is a difference in the cultures that distinguish the two worlds. In any case, Emerson's pro-Western stance is too evident to be missed: he speaks of "immovable institutions" and of a "deaf, unimplorable fate" in characterizing the Orient, but he emphasizes the "active" and "creative" in characterizing the Western mind, which clearly stands higher. And finally Europe is "a land of arts, inventions, trade, freedom. If the East loved infinity, the West delighted in boundaries" (*Works*, IV, 52).

Certainly it is not out of dislike that Emerson subordinates the Orient to the Occident; but it is specifically out of his belief in a consequential movement of history, a movement which would establish the Occident as superior and the Orient as inferior. In the "Divinity School Address" Emerson writes, suggesting: "I look for the hour when that supreme Beauty which ravished the souls of those Eastern men, and chiefly of those Hebrews, and through their lips spoke oracles to all time, shall speak in the West also. The Hebrew and Greek Scriptures contain immortal sentences, that have bread of life to millions. But they had no epical integrity; are fragmentary; are not shown in their order to the intellect. I look for the new Teacher that shall follow so far those shining laws that he shall see them come full circle."[11] In Plato Emerson saw a "new Teacher," a teacher who prefigures America's "strong man" who, in turn, "has entered the race" (*JMN*, II, 218). Thus Emerson attempts to identify himself with Plato, and his identification with the Greek philosopher implicates him in the westward movement of civilization; it suggests America's preeminence in world history, a preeminence which is part of a sequential movement that involves a transition from the Oriental to the Occidental, and from Europe to America.

Emerson's assessment of world civilization is not motivated by any kind of bias against the Orient. On the contrary, there is a strong evidence to believe that he has a unique admiration for it. The essay on "Persian Poetry," for instance, his fascination with the Sufi poets, his imitation of Hafiz and Saadi, his numerous quotations from the Qur'an and other Islamic literature, his efforts to appropriate Indian and Brahmin mythology, all suggest a uniquely sympathetic attitude.[12] In the essay on "Plato," Emerson points out that the Orient had something the Greek "Teacher" could not possess, something that kept him from influencing multitude: "It is almost the sole deduction from the merit of Plato, that his writings have not, --what is no doubt incident to this regnancy of intellect in his work,--the vital authority which the screams of prophets and the sermons of unlettered Arabs and Jews possess" (*Works*, IV, 76). Emerson was deeply attracted to the Oriental mind, to its "vital authority," unity, spirituality, and mysticism. All were among the several things that drew him toward the Orient--not as a place, but certainly as a cultural idea. But Emerson's pro-Western preference is more overt, though he grants the Orientals (Arabs, Persians, Indians) a fair position on the scale of civilization: "If it comes back to the question of final superiority," Emerson writes, "it is too plain that there is no question that the star of empire rolls West" (*Works*, X, 179). Emerson's concern here is with the superiority of an Occidental West as opposed to the inferiority of an Oriental East. Being Occidental is being better: "Orientalism is Fatalism, resignation: Occidentalism is Freedom and Will. We Occidentals are educated to wish to be first" (*JMN*, X, 90).[13] Suffice it to say that Emerson read and admired the Orientals without abandoning an awareness of his ascendency and superiority. His final verdict is "we read the Orientals, but remain Occidental" (*JMN*, XIV, 166).

In a lecture on "Natural Religion," which he read to a group of religious liberals known as "Radicals," at their meeting held in Boston in 1869, Emerson, while he discusses the doctrines of the existence of Christ, is reported in the newspapers as having said that "We measure all religions by their civilizing power. We account Mohammedanism, Mormonism, Thugism, Agapism, and other sects, old or new, which gratify the passions, as mischievous and therefore false. Christianity, on the other hand, throve against the physical interests and passions of men, and needs no other stamp of truth."[14] That the Muslim Orient is characterized by a religion which gratifies "the physical interests and passions of men" Emerson accepts at this point by ignoring the spiritual foundation of the religion, but in the same lecture he points out, somewhat apologetically, that although the "Character of Mohammed is, on the page of history, very bad," there is "a certain spiritual elevation in [the Prophet's character], which appeared in his followers. And certainly in the Koran, whether they have borrowed the Christian Scriptures or not, there is abundance of noble sentences."[15] Even though the Muslim Orient might "have borrowed the Christian Scriptures,"[16] there remains in it "abundance of noble sentences" which certainly struck Emerson's mind to the furthest extremes. Emerson's interest in the Muslim Orient, however, reveals that he was more prepared to be involved in certain manifestations of the outer form of the religion--as is indicated in specific sayings and utterances--than in its philosophical, theoretical dogmas. Thus Emerson imbued his writing with Islamic quotations, or brief, incidentally confused, references to Islamic metaphysics, and he made these subservient to his views.

In an essay on "Fate", which appeared in *The Conduct of Life* (1860), Emerson displayes his understanding of the concept at hand.

> Great men, great nations, have not been boasters and buffoons, but perceivers of the terror of life, and have manned themselves to face it. The Spartan, embodying his religion in his country, dies before its majesty without a question. The Turk, who believes his doom is written on the iron leaf in the moment when he entered the world, rushes on the enemy's sabre with undivided will. The Turk, the Arab, the Persian, accepts the foreordained fate:--

"On two days, it steads not to run from thy grave,
    The appointed, and unappointed day;
On the first, neither balm nor physician can save,
    Nor thee, on the second, the Universe slay."
              (*Works*, VI, 5)

Emerson argues to the conclusion that the doctrine of fatalism may be turned to a beneficent force, if it is properly understood. But it can also be a social evil if accepted passively or resignedly. Emerson's understanding of the concept is enhanced by the succeeding essay on "Power." The essay develops the idea of freedom overagainst surrender to fate, which to Emerson is a characteristics of the Muslim Orient: "Orientalism is Fatalism, resignation." A complete resignation to fate Emerson dismisses as distasteful. In the Preface that Emerson wrote for Saadi's *Gulistan*, in 1865, he describes the Persian poets as fatalists: "In common with his countrymen, Saadi gives prominence to fatalism, a doctrine which, in Persia, in Arabia, and in India, has had in all ages a dreadful charm. 'To all men,' says the Koran, 'is their day of death appointed, and they cannot postpone or advance it one hour.'"[17] Emerson illustrates his point with a quotation from the Qur'an which in turn expresses its fatalist nature. Emerson's argument here constitutes his own understanding of an Oriental system of determinism, a determinism which distinguishes two predestinate points in every man's life: the day of his birth and that of his death. In the essay on "Persian Poetry," Emerson characterizes the Persians, stressing their fatalism: "Religion and poetry are all their civilization. The religion teaches an inexorable destiny. It distinguishes only two days in each man's history, --his birthday, called *the Day of the Lot*, and the Day of Judgment. Courage and absolute submission to what is appointed for him are his virtues" (*Works*, VIII, 238-239).

But Emerson found much more in the Persian poets than fatalism. The Sufi poets, particularly Hafiz and Saadi,[18] influenced Emerson more profoundly than any other group of Oriental writers.[19] The affinity between Emerson's thought and the Persian poets is tangible. But his remarks on them and their poetry remain rather general. Even though he developed an ideal concept of Hafiz and Saadi, Emerson did not seem to have attempted to characterize them as poets, to see in what way, or ways, they were similar, and how they differed. Yet he admired their poetry and accepted it as ideal. And he viewed them as poets of intellectual liberty. While they believed in a designated fate, the Persian poets enjoyed an "intellectual freedom" that was part of a joyful attitude toward life (*Works*, VIII, 418). In "Fate" Emerson admires the "sallies of freedom. One example of which is the verse of the Persian Hafiz, 'Tis written on the gate of Heaven, 'Woe to him who suffers himself to be betrayed by Fate!'" (*Works,* VI, 29). And again "We learn that the soul of Fate is the soul of us, as Hafiz sings,

> "'Alas! till now I had not known,
> My guide and fortune's guide are one.'"
> (*Works*, VI, 40)

In the essay on "Persian Poetry," referring to Hafiz' "heroic sentiment and contempt for the world," Emerson writes: "And sometimes his ... world [is] only on pebble more in the eternal vortex and revolution of Fate:--

> "'I am: what I am
> My dust will be again.'"
> (*Works*, VIII, 250)

In the essay on "power," while he discusses the forms of power and the ideas of freedom, Emerson speaks of "this affirmative force.... 'On the neck of the young man,' said Hafiz, 'sparkles no gem so gracious as enterprise'" (*Works*, VI, 57). And at the end of *The Conduct of Life*, in the essay on "Illusions," Emerson writes, pointing out the charm of illusions and the necessity of recognizing them, "It would be hard to put more mental and moral philosophy than the Persians have thrown into a sentence,

> "Fooled though must be, thou wisest of the wide:
> Then be the fool of virtue, not of vice.'"
> (*Works*, VI, 325)

Undoubtedly Emerson liked this quality of freedom and mental force which the Persian poets had. Speaking of the relative recklessness toward life which they expressed in their poetry, Emerson quotes Hafiz:

> "'I batter the wheel of heaven
>   When it rolls not rightly by
> I am not one of the snivellers
>   Who fall thereon and die."
> (*Works*, VIII, 244-245)

Again:

"Loose the knots of the heart; never think on thy fate:
No Enclid has yet disentagled that snarl."
(*Works*, VIII, 246)

It is this bold, but joyful, attitude toward life that Emerson admires most; for, like Hafiz, he believed that the force of men's thoughts lies in the way of uttering them. "Loose the knots of the heart" is in effect a statement that shows the willingness of a Muslim to die when the appointed time comes.

This quality of recklessness is also a quality of rejoicing and intellectual vastness. As Emerson tells us, "Hafiz praises wine, maidens, boys, birds, mornings, and music, to give vent to his immense hilarity and sympathy with every form of beauty and joy. . . . Those are the natural topics and language of his wit and perception. But it is the play of wit and joy of song that he loves.... " (*Works*, VIII, 249-250). Emerson goes on to say, comparing Hafiz and Shakespeare, "A saint might lend an ear to the riotous fun of Falstaff; for it is not created to excite the animal appetites, but to vent the joy of the supernal intelligence" (*Works*, VIII, 250). So, in the overall analysis, the merit of expressing "the joy of supernal intelligence" becomes a "certificate of profound thought" and "intellectual liberty" (*Works*, VIII, 248). If Hafiz vented supreme joy, Saadi was "the joy-giver and the enjoyer" (*Works*, IX, 133). In the essay on "Shakespeare; or, the Poet," Emerson remarks: "One more royal trait properly belongs to the poet. I mean his cheerfulness, without which no man can be a poet,--for beauty is his aim. . . . Beauty, the spirit of joy and hilarity, he sheds over the universe. . . . Homer lies in the sunshine; Chaucer is glad and erect, and Saadi says, 'It was rumored abroad that I was penitent, but what have I to do with repentence?'" (*Works*, IV, 05-206). While he refers to Shakespeare, Homer, Dante, and Chaucer, Emerson simultaneously mentions Saadi and brings all together. If Hafiz and Shakespeare are poets of "joy" and "emancipation," Saadi was the poet of "cheerful temper," a poet in whose poetry "suns rise and set" (*Works*, IX, 134). In the poem "Saadi" Saadi emerges as "The cheerer of men's hearts" (*Works*, IX, 131). The "Wisdom of God is he" (*Works*, IX, 130). And in the Preface to *Gulistan* Emerson writes: "[Saadi] exhibits perpetual variety of situation and incident, and an equal depth of experience with Cardinal de Retz in Paris, or Doctor Johnson in London. He finds room on his narrow canvas for the extremes of the lot, the play of motives, the rule of destiny, the lessons of morals, and the portraits of great men." Emerson adds: "Though he has not the lyric flights of Hafiz, [Saadi] has wit, practical sense, and just moral sentiments. He has the instinct to teach, and from every

76

occurrence must draw the moral. . . . He is the poet of friendship, love, self-devotion, and serenity."[20] In other words, to Emerson, Saadi is a man of real genius, of morality, of "practical sense," and "just moral sentiments." He is both a teacher and a poet, an enjoyer and a joy-giver. In brief Saadi is not only a poet of "friendship" and "self-devotion," but he is also a teacher of "the lessons of morals," an example of "great men."

Emerson saw yet another feature in the Persian Saadi--Self-Reliance. Near the opening of the poem "Saadi" Emerson suggests that Saadi had such a quality.

> Yet Saadi loved the race of men,--
> No churl, immured in cave or den;
> ....
> But he has no companion;
> Come ten, or come a million,
> Good Saadi dwells alone.
> (*Works*, IX, 130)

This virtue takes on other forms in Saadi's writing as well as in that of Hafiz. It becomes an expression of self-assurance, self-independence, and authority. In the like manner Emerson writes of Hafiz: "That hardihood and self-equality of every sound nature, which result from the feeling that the spirit in him is entire and as good as the world, which entitle the poet to speak with authority, and make him an object of interest. . . . are in Hafiz, and abundantly fortify and ennoble his tone" (*Works*, VIII, 247). This feeling of self-assurance helped the Persian poets accomplish self-reliance and justify it to the common man by means of self-expression. Since, in a Sufi sense, the whole of nature evidences divinity, absolute beauty is to be reflected in all natural objects and thus in every self-reliant man, who could be a poet if he perfectly perceived the Beauty of Nature. Self-expression, then, is an utterance of every self-reliant man who could use nature as his language. Emerson wrote of Saadi: "He has also that splendor of expression which alone, without wealth of thought, sometimes constitutes a poet, and forces us to ponder the problem of style."[21] In an entry in the journals, this quality of self-expression is more clear. "Expression," writes Emerson, influenced by the reading of Hafiz, "is all we want: not knowledge, but vent: we know enough; but have not leaves and lungs enough for a healthy perspiration and growth. Hafiz has: Hafiz' good things, like those of all good poets, are the cheap blessings of water, air, and fire [the elements of Nature].... 'Keep the body open,' is the hygeian precept. . . . Large utterance!" (*JMN*, IX, 68-70). Emerson believed that for the ideal poet (the Sufi poets were generally ideal to Emerson) the splendid expression is Nature. And Nature is language, a language that the good poets alone can make and communicate to their fellow men.

To use Frederic I. Carpenter's judicious judgment, "to Hafiz and Saadi as ideal poets Emerson ascribed freedom of thought and freedom of spirit, which resulted in their feeling of absolute joy in the world; how they showed him a sincerity and self-reliance, which assured them of the basic value of life; and finally how they possessed for him a perception of beauty in Nature and in Man, which inspired their poetic expression."[22] Obviously Emerson admired and spoke well of both Hafiz and Saadi, not because they had "partially freed themselves from mohammedanism," as Carpenter explains,[23] but because they were poets of intellectual liberty, of "hilarity," of "serenity" in their own Sufi way. Although he still identified them as fatalists, Emerson, I believe, admired the Persian poets because of the quality of mental vastness they enjoyed; the variety of subjects they treated, and, more specifically, because they had a "perception of beauty in Nature and in Man." They praised "wine [wine in a Sufi sense is a symbol of intoxication with Divinity], maidens, boys, birds, mornings, and music...." (*Works*, VIII, 249-50) in expressing their love of beauty. It is the use of wit and the expression of Beauty that gave Saadi and Hafiz the assurance of pleasing the Almighty with their poetry. "Like Homer and Dante and Chaucer, Saadi [and Hafiz]," asserts Emerson, "possessed a great advantage over the poets of cultivated times in being the representatives of learning and thought to [their] countrymen. Those old poets felt that all wit was their wit, they used their memory as readily as their invention, and were at once the librarian as well as the poet, historiographer as well as the priest of the Muses" (*JMN*, IX, 38). The Sufi poets were the inspired men of their people. And they used their cultivated thought and memory and wit to demonstrate their admiration for the beautiful and, more importantly, for the divine. In "Eloquence" Emerson writes: "The Persian poet Saadi tells us that a person with a disagreeable voice was reading the Koran aloud, when a holy man, passing by, asked what was his monthly stipend. He answered, "Nothing at all.' 'But why then do you take so much trouble?' He replied, 'I read for the sake of God.' The other rejoined, 'for God's sake, do not read; for if you read the Koran in this manner you will destroy the splendor of Islamism" (*Works*, VIII, 121). And that Saadi himself wrote poetry for the sake of God is revealed when Emerson writes of the "angels descending with salvers of glory in their hands. On asking one of them for whom those were intended, he answered, 'For Shaikh Saadi of Shiraz who has written a stanza of poetry that has met with the approbation of God Almighty'" (*JMN*, IX, 39). Though fabulous, such a note shows Emerson's appreciation of the quality of eloquence which Saadi held. In much the same manner Hafiz replied to the pilgrim returning from

78

Makkah: "Boast not rashly, prince of pilgrims, of thy fortune. Thou hast indeed seen the temple; but I, the Lord of the temple. Nor has any man inhaled from the musk-bladder of the merchant or from the musky morning wind that sweet air which I am permitted to breathe every hour of the day" (*Works*, VIII, 254). Indeed in seeing, and simultaneously expressing, Beauty, Hafiz appears to have seen the Lord; and, likewise, Saadi has written a stanza of verse so eloquent that it had pleased God the Almighty.

Suffice it to say that Emerson's interest in, and admiration for, the Sufi poets are so evident that they can hardly go unnoticed. Though flattering and sympathetic as Emerson's stance toward the Muslim Orient is, it is yet imbued with certain simplifications of Islam and the Prophet. But these are only scattered, sometimes confused, remarks. As early as 1841, in an entry in the journals arguing to the conclusion that worship of saints and worship in general are diversions "from the insight of the soul", Emerson observes:

> The various matters which men magnify, as trade, law, creeds, sciences, paintings, coins, manuscripts, histories, poems, are all pieces of *virtue* which serve well enough to unfold the talents of the man, but are all diversions from the insight of the soul. Saints' worship is one of these, --the worship of Mahomet or Jesus,--like all the rest, a fine field of ingenuity wherein to construct theories....
>
> (*JMN*, VII, 452)

The quoted passage does not accurately highlight the spirit of Islam. Muhammad, like all the Muslims, worshipped and believed in *Allah*, and Emerson's comparison between the worship of Jesus in Christianity and the worship of Muhammad in Islam is untenable since it disregards the fact that the Prophet is not God and should not be worshipped. And in the essay on "Social Aims", while he discusses the bases of civil society that include social and individual manners, labor, public action, conversation, and education, Emerson points out:

> True wit never made us laugh. Mahomet seems to have borrowed by anticipation of several centuries a leaf from the mind of Swendenborg, when he wrote in the Koran:-- 'On the day of resurrection those who have indulged in ridicule will be called to the door of Paradise, and have it shut in their faces when they reach it. Again, on their turning back, they will be called to another door, and again, on reaching it, will see it closed against them; and so on *ad infinitum*, without end."
>
> (*Works*, VIII, 98)

79

While Emerson errs if he means literally that Muhammad wrote the Qur'an, he correctly perceives that the Prophet encouraged and urged the Muslims to have a sound sense of seriousness in many of his utterances and occasional remarks. The Qur'an is, of course, God's words that the Prophet, by God's decree, was to deliver to the Muslims and non-Muslims alike. In any case, Emerson found the Prophet's words congenial. And he uses them to illustrate his point that an excess of humor is incompatible with sincerity and seriousness. Again, while he attributes seriousness to the Prophet, Emerson suggest that "Mahomet seems to have borrowed by anticipation of several centuries a leaf of the mind of Swedenborg...." Such a remark, though it may not be taken literally, seems to imply that the Occident too had its own moral, religious strictness which Muhammad had anticipated. At any rate, Emerson's tendency to take the liberty of incorporating Islamic quotations and ideas into his own thought shows an interest in their inspirational and cultural value.

Discussing social laws that include labor, trade, property, and faith, in a lecture on "Man the Reformer," Emerson points out that the spread of Islam was because of the impelling power of its beliefs and its fanatical enthusiasm.

> Every great and commanding moment in the annals of the world is the triumph of some enthusiasm. The victories of the Arabs after Mahomet, who, in a few years, from a small and mean beginning, established a larger empire than that of Rome, is an example. They did they knew not what. The naked Derar, horsed on a idea, was found an overmatch for troop of Roman cavalry. The women fought like men, and conquered the Roman men. They were miserably equipped, miserably fed. They were temperance troops. There was neither brandy nor flesh needed to feed them. They conquered Asia, and Africa, and Spain, on barley.
> (*The Collected Works*, I, 157)

Indeed Islam spread in a relatively short period of time, and the Muslims conquered Asia, Africa, and Spain. But the religion had a power of faith, too, which is what Emerson means by enthusiasm, and once in the battlefield, the Muslims, though "miserably fed" and "miserably equipped," believed that the cause of God -- or, as the Qur'an puts it, the *sabil Allah* -- was well worth the struggle. To Emerson, Christendom, unlike Islam, had a less fanatic but more gracious faith, though this he criticizes as dead, moribund except in name. In the same lecture Emerson says:

80

But there will dawn ere long on our politics, on our modes of living, a nobler morning than that Arabian faith, in the sentiment of love. This is the one remedy for all ills, the panacea of nature.... This great, overgrown, dead Christendom of ours still keeps alive at least the name of a lover of mankind.
(The Collected Works, I, 158-159)

The implicit contrast between his idea of a newer faith based on a sentiment of love and Oriental Islam as well as dead Christianity reveals Emerson's distrust of the civilizing power of Islam or any other formal religion. For in the early inspiration of Christianity (now formalized and dead) he sees a "nobler morning than that Arabian faith." So if Islam suggested to Emerson an impelling enthusiasm and religious heroism, Christendom brought to mind "the name of a lover of mankind."

In an entry in his journals, which he entitles "Mahomet and Woman," Emerson brings in ideas about the transformation of Islam as a religion into practical, enthusiastic power, and he associates these ideas with a certain Mr. Vethake of New York.

Mr. V[ethake]'s opinion was that Mahomet had tried power, and Jesus, or, I think, John, persuasion; that Mahomet had felt that persuasion, this John-persuasion had miserably failed... and he said, I will try this Oriental weapon, the sword, which never, never will go West; and he said to Ayesha, "I have found out how to work it. This woman element will not bear the sword; well, I will dispose of woman: She may exist; but henceforward I will veil it." So he veiled Woman. Then the sword could work and eat. . . . I smelt fagots.... Fagots!
(*JMN*, VIII, 324)

The sword Muhammad used in much the same way as he used persuasion. But Emerson's acquaintance, Vethake, perhaps reiterating the centuries-long tradition of equating Islam with religious tyranny, viewed Muhammad as a Prophet who transformed religion into an impelling power by granting full license to the sword and by suppressing woman--the most civilizing element in society. In the passage, however, we are told that "This woman element [could] not bear the sword. . . . So he [Muhammad] veiled it." Even though this "veiled" element of society was neither disposed of, nor dismissed as incapable of "sufficient moral or intellectual force,[24] it is suggested here that such an element could be suppressed. On the contrary, in the passage which I just quoted from "Man the Reformer," Emerson

tells us that "The [Muslim] women fought like men, and conquered Roman men."
The view which Emerson held there is obviously at variance with Vethake's, in
that it shows more admiration for this sense of enthusiasm he found in Islam than
distrust.

By and large, however, Emerson found the Muslim Orient congenial. His
fascination for, as well as criticism of, the Muslim East may perhaps be explained
as stemming from a mixture of condescension and admiration. Emerson read the
Orientals, and used all his reading in his writings, but he still identified his
thought closely with the Western World. He read them in order to get a vocabulary for his ideas (he did not want to get the Oriental ideas for their own sake).[25]
In other words, Emerson preferred to remain Occidental. And his interest in
Oriental philosophy and religions remains a manifestation of a lightly prejudice-
colored but preeminently sympathetic attitude, a demonstration of the western
preeminence in world history. What Emerson wanted to do was to transform the
Orient into a framework, or rather a vocabulary, of his own. Admittedly he was
successful in incorporating the Oriental material as an exotic element, and, on
occasion, as in the case of the Sufi poets, he showed a profound interest in, and
fascination for, the Sufi ideals in their own right.

II

Contemporary with Emerson, John Greenleaf Whittier, not concerned primarily with Islam and the Muslims or their philosophy and literature, illustrates yet
another use of the Muslim Orient. "But since Whittier's interest [in the Orient]
cannot be totally separated from any transcendentalist's interest," as Arthur
Christy perceptively observes, "it is well to note that the contrast between the
Emersonian attitude and Whittier's was the contrast between the liberalism and
the Quaker orthodoxy of the time. This was reflected not only in the theology of
the men, but also in the literary use they made of [Oriental] material."[26] Some of
Whittier's poems, as will be indicated, have pseudo-Oriental settings and themes
and others have general and inexact allusions to the Muslim Orient. In "The
Orientalism of Whittier," Arthur Christy indicates that he had examined Whittier's
library and found a number of Oriental books which afforded Whittier a general
exposition of the Orient.[27] Christy also argues that Whittier knew Hafiz and the
Sufi poets in general, the *Arabian Nights*, the *Travels of Ibn Batuta*, and that he
read the Qur'an. But evidence to indicate exactly how Whittier secured access to
the Orientalism that sprang up in his poetry remains lacking.[28] Whittier, however,
acknowledges a debt to a friend and fellow poet, Bayard Taylor, for having

introduced him to Oriental themes and ideas, or for having at least been one medium through which he knew the Orient. In "Bayard Taylor," Whittier says of his friend:

> He brought us wonders of the new and old;
> We shared all climes with him. The Arab's tent
> To him its story-telling secret lent.
> And, pleased, we listened to the tales he told.
> (p. 212)[29]

But insofar as Taylor is an influence, we shall later see it was a highly romantic, if somewhat inaccurate, source.

Often Whittier, as in "The Cypress-Tree of Ceylon", starts with or refers to a passage in Oriental literature, which he restates or reworks briefly, and concludes with a Christian moral, and my purpose is to see how he uses moral themes with regard to the Muslim Orient. "The Cypress-Tree" is introduced by the following prose passage: "Ibn Batuta, the celebrated Mussulman traveler of the fourteenth century, speaks of a cypress-tree in Ceylon, universally held sacred by the natives, the leaves of which were said to fall only at certain intervals, and he who had the happiness to find and eat one of them was restored, at once, to youth and vigor. The traveler saw several venerable Jogees, or saints, sitting silent and motionless under the tree." After this comes a description in verse of the pious men sitting beneath the tree as they wait for the fall of the restorative leaf.

> They sat in silent watchfulness
>   The sacred cypress-tree about,
> And, from beneath old wrinkled brows,
>   Their failing eyes looked out.
> Gray Age and sickness waiting there
> Through weary night and lingering day,--
>   (p. 14)

The description of the venerable Jogees is followed by the question:

> What was the world without to them?
>   The Moslem's sunset call, he dance
> Of Ceylon's maids, the passing gleam
>   Of battle-flag and lance?
>   (p. 14)

Certainly not. Whittier concludes with a prayer, characteristic of his verse, to the Saviour who rose from the redeeming death to wake his slumbering disciples:

> Bend o'er now, as over them,
> > And set our sleep-bound spirit free
> Nor leave us slumbering in the watch
> > Our souls should keep with Thee!
> > > (p. 14)

Thus Whittier, in a didactic manner, used an old tale of pagan belief to underscore the better efficacy of Christian faith.

In "Skipper Ireson's Ride" Whittier rewords a story which registers the wrath of the people of Marblehead toward a certain captain, Ireson, who was said to have abandoned his sinking ship. In the poem, the tarred and feathered captain is driven through the streets of Marblehead by the enraged populace. The ballad opens incongrously as the strangeness of Ireson's ride out of Marblehead is compared to other famous rides of story. The reference to Apuleius's journey after his transformation into an ass, to Muhammad's flight on the back of al-Buraq, and to the Tartar King's ride on a magical horse sets a grotesque, grimly mocking tone for the poem.

> Of all the rides since the birth of time,
> Told in story or sung in rhyme,--
> On Apuleius's Golden Ass,
> Or one-eyed Calender's horse of brass,
> Witch astride of a human back,
> Islam's Prophet on Al-Borak,--
> The strangest ride that ever was sped
> Was Ireson's, out from Marblehead!
> > Old Floyd Ireson, for his hard heart,
> > Tarred and feathered and carried in a cart
> By the women of Marblehead!
> > (p. 55)

By implicitly comparing Ireson's ride to Muhammad's, Whittier puts Ireson side by side with the Prophet, mixing thus the secular with the religious. The juxtaposition of the two rides suggests that they are at the same level of reality, even if Ireson's seems to be much more believable to Whittier than the Prophet's. Be this as it may, Muhammad claimed, and the Muslims believe, that he rode al-

Buraq on the night of his ascension, *Miradj*.[30] But Whittier's point is to say that Ireson's ride was as strange as other famous rides in history, hence the reference to the Prophet which he might have employed for the mere expression of the exotic. Though it may be exotic, the Prophet's departure from the earth to heaven cannot be regarded as similar to Ireson's flight from Marblehead. But Whittier wanted to present a moral idea, an illustration of "Christian democracy,"[31] as becomes clear at the end of the poem where the people accept Ireson's plea of remorse and suffering.

In "Miriam," while it alludes to the Qur'an, the discussion between Whittier and a friend, after they had left the Quaker meeting-house in a sombre Sabbath mood, turned to the question of God's essential nature and benevolence toward humanity.

> "Truth is one;
> And, in all lands beneath the sun,
> Whose hath eyes to see may see
> The tokens of its unity.
> No scroll of creed its fullness wraps,
> We trace it not by school-boy maps,
> Free as the sun and air it is
> Of latitudes and boundaries.
> In Vedic verse, in dull Koran,
> Are messages of good to man; ..."
> (p. 95)

To support his reasoning that "Truth is one," Whittier points out that in "Vedic verse," "dull Koran," and "the slant-eyed sages of Cathy" is evidence of its oneness. Here it should be pointed out at the outset that Whittier has no factual knowledge of the Qur'an, that he believes it to be tedious and boring, repeating thus the long-accepted view of the Qur'an as dull, which George Sale had originated. In turn, Whittier complements the image of the period by continuing a common tradition accepted at the time, a tradition which the contemporary larger movement of the English romanticists (Lord Byron, Thomas Moore, and Robert Southey--to name only a few) had maintained. Admittedly, Whittier might have read Sale's unreliable translation of the Qur'an, as Christy suggests, and that made him hold such an opinion of it and know it as a tedious "book." Later in the poem, however, to affirm his view that differing faiths "agree in one sweet law of charity" (p. 96), Whittier tells of a tale "not found in printed books,--in sooth,/ A fancy, with slight hint of truth" (p. 96). The tale is concerned with a dedicated

Christian woman, Miriam, who uses Christian doctrines to quell the rage of a "heathen" king (the king, a certain Shah Akbar, turns out to be a Muslim). Wanting to exchange views with Miriam, the king says:

> "Tell me, O Miriam, something thou hast read
> In childhood of the Master of thy faith,
> Whom Islam also owns. Our Prophet saith:
> 'He was a true apostle, yea, a Word
> And spirit sent before me from the Lord.'"
> (p. 96)

Consequently, as Miriam begins to tell "of the all-loving Christ," the king becomes more convinced that

> "Something of this large charity I find
> In all the sects that sever humankind."
> (p. 97)

As the tale unfolds itself further, we realize that one of the king's hareem falls in love with a slave. And

> . . . a murmur through the hareem ran
> That one, recalling in her dusky face
> The full-lipped, milk-eyed beauty of a race
> Known as the blameless Ethiops of Greek song,
> Plotting to do her royal master wrong,
> Now waited death at the great Shah's command.
> (p. 97)

But Christian Miriam immediately draws a moral lesson for the Muslim king, reminding him of the words of his Prophet: "'Whoso doth endure/ And pardon, of eternal life is sure?'" Eventually softened by a storm of passions, the king becomes so forgiving.

> "They [the slaves] sinned through love,
>   as I through love forgive:
> Take them beyond my realm, but let them live!"
> (p. 98)

The poem ends with a Christian moral of love, an acceptable Islamic idea as well.

86

In the "Christian Slave" there is another moral. Here Whittier imagines a slave auction at which a good Christian woman is on the stand for sale. The point of the poem is to say that the Christian church is at fault in not fighting the evils of human society, and especially slavery, and Whittier's illustration is to say even worse is Islam in this respect.

> Oh, shame! the Moslem thrall,
> Who, with his master, to the Prophet kneels,
> While turning to the sacred Kebla feels
> His fetters break and fall.
> (p. 289).

Now in Islam Muhammad, whom Whittier is even unable to think of as anything other than a "false prophet,"[32] wields no special powers and claims no superiority to man other than the distinction of having been chosen by *Allah* to deliver a divine message. For a Muslim to pray and "kneel" to the prophet is as grave a matter as abolishing the church or denying the divinity of Jesus in Christianity. Whittier indicates that the "Moslem thrall," while restrained in fetters, kneels to the Prophet together with his master. Such an act is certainly appalling to modern readers, Christian and Muslim alike; for buying and selling human beings is indefensible by any stretch of the imagination, a theme repeatedly emphasized in Whittier's poetry. This is presumably why Islam interdicts slavery.

In a letter to Edna Dean Proctor, Whittier praises General Gordon's "brave" endeavor to abolish slavery in, and to pacify the populace of, the Sudan. But, as a poet, Whittier has other concerns as well:

> What a place for an artist the Soudan would be--if an artist were sure of keeping his head on his shoulders? Those fierce wild hordes--in all variety of costume and color, with their shields of hippopotamus hides, their long spears, and battle axes... --the strange desert scenery, and relentless sun would be rare subjects for his pencil. I suppose thee can form some idea of it, from having looked on the Meccan Caravan at Cairo.[33]

The Sudan strikes Whittier's attention as a "rare subject" which can both serve the artist's purpose and satisfy the taste of a reading public. Viewed as a place where an artist can find exotic material for "his pencil," the Sudan becomes something of a romantic reach, something an artist might capture: "costume," "color," "desert scenery," "wild hordes," "spears," and "axes." So the romantic goes side by side with the moral, as we can see.

Whittier's incidental use of, and passing reference to, the Muslim Orient is, however, shown in poems which contain stereotypical images of the Arabo-Islamic. Whittier, as in "Derne," thinks of the Arab as something that recalls a "tent." In the poem, the two words "Arab" and "tent" appear to be used interchangeably. This is not to imply that "tent" means "Arab," but it seems to suggest that the word (tent), being the common poetic device of metaphor, evoked an image of the Arab in Whittier's mind. For instance:

> The sounds of Moslem life are still;
> No mule-bell tinkles down the hill;
> Stretched in the broad court of the Khan,
> The dusty Bornou caravan
> Lies heaped in slumber, beast and man,
> The sheik is dreaming in his tent,
> His noisy Arab tongue o'erspent;
> (p. 311)[34]

The poem, though essentially concerned with the practices of slavery in the city of Derne, contains a description of "the city of the Moor," and various references to the "Moslem life" are incorporated in stereotypes: "the mule-bell," "the Khan," "the dreaming sheik," the "tent," and the "noisy Arab tongue." And in "The Hachish" there is another stereotype of the Arab.

> The Arab by his desert well
> Sits choosing from some Caliph's daughters,
> And hears his single camel's bell
> Sound welcome to his regal quarters
> The Koran's reader makes complaint
> Of Shitan dancing on and off it;
> The robber offers alms, the Saint
> Drinks Tokay and blasphemes the Prophet.
> (p. 317).

The poem treats of the Oriental plant of the Hashish; the bad effects that follow upon its eating and the evil "scenes that it awakes." The quoted passage shows one of the scenes which bears reference to Islam and the Muslims. At the outset, it should be pointed out that Islam not only interdicts Hashish and the like plants (even alcohol for this matter), but it also incurs severe punishment on those who eat, sell or buy it. It seems to me that Whittier's view here exhibits something very much like what one might call cultural misconception: for he appears to conceive of the Muslim Orient as a world in which wrong doings might be indulged with no social consequences or moral qualms. While he pictures "the Arab ... choosing from the Caliph's daughters," Whittier simultaneously refers to "the Koran's reader," who is making "complaint of shitan [i.e. Satan]." Certainly Whittier has a moral point here, and his illustration is to say that, compared with Christianity, even worse could the case be in Islam. In harmony with Whittier's generally censorious attitude toward the Muslim Orient are the following lines from a letter Whittier addressed to an unidentified correspondent, whom he wanted to see at his house. The letter reads: "I am sorry that thy health is not stronger, but glad it is gaining. What a pity that we have to *think* so much! I almost envy the Turk with his pipe enjoying his *Kef* [i.e., absent-mindedness, intoxication, ecstacy] and letting the world and all that is therein go by as a matter in which he is not concerned."[35] As the opposed "think" and "Kef" indicate, the idea of Oriental calm suggested here brings on negative associations: the Turk is presented as unconcerned about the world, enjoying his *Kef*, while, unlike the Turk, Whittier's friend, as indicated in the passage, is more worried about it.

Even though Whittier seems to be very little concerned about Islam and the Muslims except incidentally, he shared in the general preoccupation with the Muslim Near East manifest on the American literary scene during the nineteenth century. As could be expected, Whittier presents an unflattering picture of Islam probably because he had little knowledge of it, and because of the lack of authentic, accurate information concerning the Muslims and their religion in general. Whittier's main concern, however, was moral. What he wanted to do in many of his poems was to help his fellow men, Christian and Muslim alike, maintain and enjoy their freedom. Thus he attacked the evils of society--mainly those of slavery--and emphasized the need for equality among men. His illustration was that the Christian church is at fault in not fighting evil doings, and so in Islam. On the whole, Whittier "was a humanitarian," to use Arthur Christy's judicious words, "tolerant and kindly in spirit, who took from the stream of Oriental influences.... But he never relinquished the Christian spectacles through which he read."[36] Indeed the ethical, humanitarian element which underlies Whittier's poetry never fails to strike one's attention, but it is occasionally colored by certain cultural misconceptions or stereotypes.

Notes

1 See, on this point, Carl T. Jackson, *The Oriental Religions and American Thought: Nineteenth-Century Explorations* (Westport, Conn.: Greenwood Press, 1981). The book attempts to establish the beginnings and rise of America's discovery of the Asian religions--particularly of Hinduism, Buddhism, and of Confucianism. The book suggests that American interest in Oriental though is certainly not a passing fad. Americans began to discover Far-Eastern religion as early as the 1700s, and during the nineteenth century, with the emergence of the transcendental explorations, this interest exploded. Jackson limits the term "Oriental religion" to the religions of the Far East, mainly those of India, China and Japan, and he excludes Islam and other religions of Western Asia.

2 Ralph L. Rusk, ed. *The Letters of Ralph Waldo Emerson,* 6 vols. (New York: Columbia University Press, 1939), I, 116-117.

3 Frederic I. Carpenter, *Emerson and Asia* (Cambridge: Harvard University Press, 1930), pp. 3-4. This will henceforth be cited as *Emerson and Asia.*

4 William H. Gilman, et al., ed. *The Journals and Miscellaneous Notebooks of Ralph Waldo Emerson,* 16 vols. (Cambridge, Mass.: The Belknap Press of Harvard University, 1960-1982), I, 72. Subsequent references in the text refer to this edition; henceforth cited as *JMN.*

5 Arthur Christy, *The Orient in American Transcendentalism: A Study of Emerson, Thoreau, and Alcott* (New York: Columbia University Press, 1932), p. 68; henceforth cited as *The Orient in American Transcendentalism.*

6 *Emerson and Asia,* p. 9.

7 In 1837 Emerson lists the *Historia Muslemica* of Abdulfeda, and, in 1840, Simon Ockley's *History of the Saracens.* In 1841 he read Thomas Carlyle's book *On Heroes and Hero Worship* (which included a lecture on the Prophet). And in 1845 he read *Akhlaqe Jalali,* an interesting book which shows how Greek philosophy was introduced into Islamic mysticism. And, as early as 1822, Emerson read the *Arabian Nights,* and at the same time he was reading Gibon's *Decline and Fall of the Roman Empire,* Chapters 50 to 52 of which describe the rise and fall of the Muslim Caliphate.

8 "Emerson's Debt to the Orient," *The Monist,* 38 (Jan. 1928): 44.

9 *Emerson and Asia,* p. 14.

10 Edward W. Emerson, ed. *The Complete Works of Ralph Waldo Emerson*, 12 vols. (Boston: Houghton Mifflin, 1903-1904), IV, 39. Unless otherwise indicated, subsequent references in the text are to this edition: hereafter cited as *Works*.

11 Robert E. Spiller, et al., ed. *The Collected Works of Ralph Waldo Emerson* (Cambridge, Mass.: Harvard University Press, 1971), I, 92-93; henceforth cited as *The Collected Works*.

12 In 1850 Emerson began to keep a separate journal entitled "The Orientalist" where he entered, observes Carpenter, "the philosophy of India, the poetry of Persia and Arabia, and the wisdom of all the Oriental countries at once. And from this source he drew much of the richness which he was to put into his later essays." *Emerson and Asia*, p. 22.

13 In another entry in the journals Emerson writes: "with our Saxon education and habit of thought we all require to be first. Each man must somehow think himself the first in his own career" (*JMN*, IX, 218-219).

14 Clarence Gohdes, ed. *Uncollected Lectures by Ralph Waldo Emerson* (New York: William E. Rudge, 1932), p.54.

15 *Ibid.*, p. 60.

16 Emerson's skepticism toward Islam was typical of the time. Writing to Emerson, Thomas Carlyle, in a letter after the conclusion of the series "On Heroes," singles out the lecture on Muhammad for special mention and describes the effect on his audience. "The lecture on Mahomet ["The Hero as Prophet"] astonished my worthy friends beyond measure. It seems then this Mahomet was not a quack? Not a bit of him! That he is a better Christian, with his 'bastard Christianity,' than the most of us shovelhatted?" *The Correspondence of Emerson and Carlyle*, ed. Joseph Slater (New York: Columbia University Press, 1964), p. 274. The lecture, published in London in 1841, was praised as a fair treatment of the Prophet. It was not. But Carlyle attempted to overcome all prejudices, and to enter with sympathetic imagination into the subject. Carlyle's final verdict on the Prophet is: sincere but "he is by no means the truest of Prophets."

17 *The Gulistan; or, Rose Garden of Saadi*, trans. Francis Gladwin (Boston: Ticknor and Fields, 1865), p. ix.

18 Saadi, or Sadi, was born at Shiraz in A.D. 1194; the epithet Shirazi applies equally to him and to Hafiz, as much honored natives of that Dar al Ulum, or seat of learning. Saadi's proper name was Muslihuddin, or the Reformer of the faith, though he was better known afterwards by that of Sheikh Saadi

Shirazi: Saadi properly signifying felicity. A Sufi of profound learning, Saadi was both a poet and a philosopher, or master in every branch of science, and accomplished in the polite arts and mysticism. For a length of time he led the life of a traveler. He had visited North Africa, Abyssinia, Egypt, Syria, Palestine, Armenia, Asia Minor, and every province of Iran, and had often traveled on foot to Makkah to make pilgrimage. Saadi's work consists of a wide range of books, twenty-two in all. Of these books, six, including *The Gulistan*, a book of ethics and rules for conduct in life, are prose; the rest poetry: elegies, ghazals, and odes. And Hafiz, Shams al-Din Muhammad Shirazi, born in 1320, was lyric poet and panegyrist; and commonly considered in Persia as the pre-eminent master of the *ghazal*, a literary form generally equated with the lyric. In youth he earned the title *hafiz* (Qur'an-Memorizer), which became his pen-name, and his poetry proves that he acquired a competence in all the Muslim sciences taught in his day. Though credited with learned works in prose, his fame rests entirely on his *Diwan*, a book of mystical verses or lyrics that demonstrates his doctrine of intellectual Sufism; a doctrine of absolute surrender to the Infinite and to the overwhelming forces of the Soul. The two poets had a tremendous reputation not only in Persia, but also in the rest of the Muslim world. Their Sufi school of thought was in itself a movement that flourished in Islamic literature and philosophy, and became characteristic of "liberal" expression; liberal in that it ran against literary norms of the day.

19 Emerson wrote two essays and two poems dealing with Persian poets and poetry. The most important among these pieces is the essay on "Persian Poetry" included in *Letters and Social Aims*. Second is his poem "Saadi," first published in *The Dial*. Third is the preface to the first American edition of Saadi's *Gulistan* (1865). And finally is the idealized interpretation of Hafiz and Saadi in "Fragments on the Poet and the Poetic Gift." Emerson also translated Persian poetry from Von Hammer Purgstall, some of which is published in the Centenary Edition (*Works*, IX, 298-305). However, see for a general introduction to Emerson's debt to Persian philosophy and mysticism Mansur Ekhtiar's *Emerson and Persia* (Tehran: Tehran University Press, 1976). Ekhtiar looks mainly at Emerson's increasing interest in the Persian poets' mysticism, discussing briefly such concepts as Sufism and other doctrines Emerson found in Muslim Persia. Also see J.D. Yohannan's "Emerson's Translations of Persian Poetry from German Sources," *American Literature* 14 (1942-1943): 407-420, and "The Influence of Persian Poetry upon Emerson's Work, "*American Literature* 15 (1943-1944): 25-41. The articles indicate the number of translations of Persian poetry from German

sources, and discuss the nature of the influence of those translations in Emerson's work. Also helpful and much more broad in scope is Farida Hellal's dissertation "Emerson's Knowledge an Use of Islamic Literature," University of Houston 1971. The dissertation investigates mainly Emerson's reading in Muslim Near Eastern literature and his use of the Qur'an and Persian poetry.

20 *Gulistan,* pp. v-vii.

21 *Ibid.,* p. ix.

22 *Emerson and Asia,* p. 179.

23 *Ibid.,* 171.

24 In the essay on "Woman," read before the Woman's Rights Convention, held in Boston in 1855, Emerson criticizes "Mahomet's opinion that women have not a sufficient moral or intellectual force to control the perturbations of their physical structure" (*Works,* XI, 417).

25 See *JMN,* V, 343.

26 "Orientalism in New England: Whittier," *American Literature* 1 (1929-1930): 372.

27 See "The Orientalism of Whittier," *American Literature* 5 (1933-1934): 247-257. According to Christy books such as W.R. Alger's *Poetry of the Orient,* R.H. Stoddard's *The Book of the East,* R.S. Watson's *A Journey to Wazan, the Sacred City of Morocco,* Lydia Maria Child's *The Progress of Religious Ideas,* and Charles Dudley Warner's *In The Levant* were on the shelves of Whittier's library. Whittier also read in the files of the *Journal of the Asiatic Society of Bengal.* Also, for a brief discussion of Oriental literature and its hold on Whittier's imagination, see John A. Pollard's *John Greenleaf Whittier: Friend of Man* (Boston: Houghton Mifflin, 1949), pp. 345-349.

28 Christy argues that Sir Edwin Arnold, author of *The Light of Asia,* might have introduced Whittier to the subject, or at least was one medium through which Whittier knew it. However, Christy does not have evidence for this point. See "Orientalism in New England."

29 This and all subsequent excerpts hereon refer to *The Poetical Works of Whittier,* ed. Hyatt H. Wagoner (Boston: Houghton Mifflin, 1975). Page reference is given in the text in parentheses. As will be indicated in the next chapter, Taylor traveled extensively in Eastern countries and published in

quick succession *A Journey to Central Africa* (1854), *The Lands of the Saracen* (1855), and *Poems of the Orient.* (1855).

30 Allusion is made in the Qur'an to a vision which the Prophet had in which he seemed to be borne from Makkah to Jerusalem and hence to heaven. The word *Buraq* connotes lightning or miraculous speed.

31 In a letter to James Russel Lowell Whittier writes that the poem "has at least the merit of presenting American ideas--and the philosophy of Christian democracy." He adds "It [the poem] pleases me.... What is thy decision as to Capt. Ireson? It occurs to me that .... Mahomet mounting on Al-Borak should read 'Islam's Prophet on Al-Borak'." Quotation follows *The Letters of John Greenleaf Whittier*, ed. John B. Pickard (Cambridge: Harvard University Press, 1975), II, 346. Henceforth cited as *Letters*. Whittier prefers to use "Islam's prophet on Al-Borak" because it is a better line.

32 *Letters*, I, 450.

33 *Letters*, III, 484.

34 See also pp. 212, 313, 317, 438 in *The Poetical Works*. The prose passage that introduces the poem, "Derne," refers to the storming of the city of Derne in North Africa, in 1805, by General Eaton, an act which was "one of those feasts of hardihood and daring which have in all ages attracted the admiration of the multitude." William Eaton, the United States Counsul at Tunis, conceived the idea of removing the threat of the Barbary pirates by setting up a puppet government in Tripoli favourable to the United States. The American navy had been waging a desultory war with the Tripolitan corsairs since 1801 when Eaton, in 1803, persuaded President Jefferson to let him lead an overland expedition against Tripoli. His object was to place Hamet Karamanli on the throne of Tripoli from which he had been removed by a usurping brother. Eaton organized an army in Egypt, marched across the desert and captured Derna. The heroic action of Eaton's gave the United States Marine Corps the phrase "to the shores of Tripoli" in their official song. The expedition had an important influence in establishing American prestige in Barbary, and the fall of Derna marks a turning point in American relations with all of the North African States. Whittier incorporates the action into verse as part of his moral war against the vice of slavery.

35 *Letters*, II, 461.

36 "Orientalism in New England," *AL* 1 (1929-30): 392.

The interest of Americans in the land of the oldest civilizations has greatly increased ..., and literature relating to the Orient is in more demand than at any previous time.

Charles Dudley Warner,
My Winter on the Nile

Some men may read this who are in want of a sensation. If they love the odd and picturesque, if they loved the *Arabian Nights* in their youth, let them book themselves on board of the Peninsular and Oriental vessels, and try one dip into Constantinople or Smyrna. Walk into the bazaar and the East is unveiled to you: how often and often you have tried to fancy this .... It is wonderful too, how like it is: you may imagine that you have been in the place before, you seem to know it so well.

Thackeray, *The Journey from Cornhill to Grand Cairo*

Chapter Four :

An Observant Eye on the Muslim Orient:
American Travelers in the Levant

For the interpretation of the Muslim Orient to nineteenth-century America, especially on the level of popular interest, few agents were more important than the traveler. Traveling in the Levant aroused a large number of Americans in the nineteenth century. The quest for trade and empire, the rise of the missionary movement, and curiosity about the exotic and the outlandish, all of these induced a growing number of adventurous, and sometimes evangelical, spirits to acquire detailed and immediate acquaintance of the countries and the peoples of the Muslim East.[1] The reading public wanted information about strange places and none seemed stranger than the Levant, and the public's interest encouraged travel writing. Perhaps, as Ahmed M. Metwalli points out, "The 'cultural' orientation of the age was responsible for the increased production and dissemination of books of travel. During the nineteenth century, almost every literate and zealous traveler managed to avail himself of one or more, and sometimes all, public media, to excite, entertain, or instruct the masses with his own experiences in foreign lands. Public lectures in the increasingly popular Lyceums, serialized travel letters, serialized articles, and books were available organs of expression. the romantic adventurer, the explorer, the missionary, the merchant or merchantile, the diplomatic and military envoy, as well as the man of letters, were all able to reach and influence the public in one way or another."[2] Indeed the literate American at the beginning of the nineteenth century had few detailed accounts of the Levant and its peoples, and what he had was a romantic picture that had long struck his imagination. Thus he framed to himself a deep azure sky, alluring atmosphere; associated luxurious ease with coffee-houses and Turkish baths. He perceived the cross-legged, turbaned Turks sitting on Persian carpets, and harems sitting under palmtrees; he saw Turks and Arabs enjoying their *Keif*, or more often smoking hashish; he pictured tents, camels, and Bedouins. Such a colored picture provided a sort of Arabian-Night spell to the public, and for a long time the Levant remained an almost irresistible romantic attraction. For it had the fascination of the strange, the fascination of a different and rather fabulous world. To be sure, the Levant had always represented limitless opportunity for the special adventure of sight-seeing as it became accessible to American travelers. But even when Americans actually went to the East they selected "what they saw and ignor[ed] what did not fit in with their preconceived picture [of it]," as Maxime Rodinson suggests.[3] Thus the travelers, instead of actually observing the Muslim Orient, brought home a preconceived image, more or less; they in varying degrees added no particular information of a specific, differentiating kind, but, though sometimes fanciful, they popularized the Muslim East, and the travel book assumed an important place as a popular type of informative literature.

It would be natural to say that many of the numerous people visiting the Orient should feel impelled to publish accounts of their travel, and because of the strange and exotic nature of the Muslim East it offered to American travelers an especially rich field for comment and description. The nineteenth century, in particular, witnessed the publication of a stream of travel books, which, as a group, covered almost every aspect of life in the Levant: history, religion, manners, customs, dress, architecture, justice, government, and climate. The material and interpretation that appeared in the travel books not only captured the imagination of the reading public, but in addition they created a large body of fiction and other imaginative writing for which the Muslim Orient is the theme or background. Such literature includes, as examples, William Starbuck Mayo's *Kaloolah* (1849) and *The Berber* (1850), William Ware's *Zenobia; or, the Fall of Palmyra* (1850), Sylvanus Cobb's *Ben Hamed: The Children of Fate* (1863), Mayne Reid's *The Boy Slaves* (1864), Jaoquin Miller's *Song of the Sun Lands* (1873), Richard Henry Stoddard's *The Book of the East* (1871), to mention only a few works.

However, for most American travelers going to the Muslim East was not an end in itself, nor was the acquisition of learning a principal object. Their eyes were fixed upon the Holy Land, led partly by love of adventure, but chiefly by a pious curiosity, by an ineradicable desire to know more about the land that witnessed the birth of Jesus Christ. Yet they also wanted to satisfy their curiosity concerning the region and simultaneously to entertain the credulous public with Muslim manners and mores--and saw many other things along the way. The fruits of their explorations appeared in the numerous books covering their experiences in the Levant. The second half of the nineteenth century actually witnessed a high tide for books on the region, as described by Americans who visited it. These books include, among others, Jesse A. Spencer's *The East: Sketches of Travel in Egypt and the Holy Land* (1850), John Thomas' *Travels in Egypt and Palestine* (1853), Henry M. Harman's *A Journey to Egypt and the Holy Land* (1873), Thomas W. Knox's *Backsheesh; or, Life and Adventures in the Orient* (1875), Thomas G. Appleton's *A Nile Journal* (1876), Henry C. Potter's *The Gates of the*

East (1877), Samuel C. Bavtlett's *From Egypt to Palestine through Sinai* (1879), Edward E. Hale's *A Family Flight over Egypt and Syria* (1882), Nathan Hubbell's *My Journey to Jerusalem* (1890), and Edward G. Read's *A Domine in Bible Lands* (1894). The travelers emphasized in such accounts many of the dominant ideas which were then current at home; the popularity of travel books in turn reinforced the vogue of these ideas, and the authentic background of these books was largely influenced by the desire to communicate information and firsthand observations or impressions. The fact that travel books contained information of various kinds gave them popularity, and the element of authenticity was enhanced by the personal approach employed by many travelers in the retelling of their experiences, but often enough these experiences were exaggerated to satisfy the reader's taste for the romantic and the adventurous. In short, the Levant was, for various reasons, a favorite place for many Americans to travel in and write about, and there developed a fairly large body of literature very frequently based on personal experiences in the region, and what was written was intended as useful knowledge or information for the reader. Let us see now how the travelers characterized the East in their writings, and how their firsthand observation changed, if at all, the traditional, preconceived conception of the Muslim Near Orient that was born out of the unflattering image which the American imagination had for long entertained of the region.

As early as 1833, Nathaniel Parker Willis, an accomplished poet and a journalist, joined a cruise of the Mediterranean aboard the U.S. frigate *Constellation,* setting sail for the Levant. He arrived in Constantinople, Turkey. Determined to write a description of the region, for five weeks he took notes. While he lived among the people of Constantinople, he made sketches, wrote letters, and the result of his sojourn was the popular two-volume *Pencillings by the Way* that appeared in 1836. The book was preceded by a wide range of travel accounts written by Americans concerning American activities in the Levant: John Martin Baker's *A View of the Commerce of the Mediterranean (*1819), Josiah Brewer's *A Residence at Constantinople in the Year 1827* (1830), Henry A.V. Post's *A Visit to Greece and Constantinople* (1830), Enoch Cobb Wines' *Two Years and a Half in the Navy; or, a Journal of a Cruise in the Mediterranean and Levant* (1832), David Porter's *Constantinople and Its Environs, by an American* (1835), and George Jones' *Excursions to Cairo, Jerusalem, Damascus, and Balbec* (1836), to mention a few, and among these Willis' is the most popular and most interesting.

Pencillings by the Way is a series of letters in which Willis describes glimpses of Turkish life, manners, and customs, and views of Constantinople itself:

The world contains nothing like Constantinople. If we could compel all our senses into one, and live by the pleasures of the eye, it were a paradise transcended. The Bosphorus--the superb, peculiar incomparable Bosphorus! the dream-like, fairy built Seraglio! the sights within the city so richly strange, and the valleys and streams around it so exquisitely fair, the voluptuous softness of the dark eyes haunting every step on shore, and the spirit-like swiftness and elegance of your darting caique upon the waters! In what land is the priceless sight a treasure? Where is the fancy so delicately and divinely pampered?[4]

The bizarre and the faraway romantic appeal, the visual impressions, and the "pleasures of the eye" which this passage contains were intended to invoke exoticism in the reader's mind. Even though careful and precise in his detailed, if somewhat rapturous, descriptions of the patterns of life of the Turkish society, Willis could not resist making broad generalizations about the Turkish people, especially in his description of the Turkish mode of life and architecture. "The Turks," according to Willis, "live differently from every other people .... You walk through their town and see every individual in it, except perhaps the women of Pasha. Their houses are square boxes, the front side of which lifts on a hinge in the day-time, exposing the whole interior, with its occupants squatted in the corners or on the broad platform where their trades are followed. They are scarce larger than boxes in the theatre, and the roof projects into the middle of the street, meeting that of opposite neighbor, so that the pavement between is always dark and cool. The three or four Turkish towns I have seen have the appearance of Cabins thrown up hastily after a fire. You would not suppose they were intended to last more than a month at the farthest" (II, 42-43). Willis, as this passage suggests, appears to be censorious not only of the Turkish mode of life, but also of the Turkish architecture itself, and thus he views the Turks as different "from every other people," presumably because they did not conform to his Western rearing.

With a wealth of illustrative detail, Willis' appraisal of the conditions under which the Turkish populace live sometimes edges into humorous hyperbole. Commenting on Turkish women, Willis writes: "The women of Constantinople, I am told, almost live on confectionery. They eat incredible quantities. The Sultan's eight hundred wives and women employ five hundred cooks, and consume *two thousand five hundred pounds of sugar daily*! It is probably the most expensive item of the Seraglio kitchen" (II, 56-57). And the Turkish women could also be a subject of romantic curiosity. "It is strange," writes Willis, "how universal is the beauty of the Eastern eye. I have looked in vain hitherto for a small or unexpressive one. It is quite startling to meet the gaze of such large liquid orbs, bent upon you from their silken fringes, with the unwinking steadiness of look common to the female of this country" (II, 55). Though rapturously romantic such a depiction is, Willis goes on with his exaggerated descriptions of Constantinople and its people throughout the book. He relates his experiences at the Turkish baths, bazaars, palaces, cafes, and mosques, and he comments on the condition of the dogs of Constantinople as it appeared to him. "I had heard," says Willis, "that the dogs of Constantinople knew and hated a Christian. By the time I reached the middle of the square, a wretched puppy at my heels had succeeded in announcing the presence of a stranger. They were upon me in a moment from every heap of garbage ... when an old Turk ... came kindly to my relief" (II, 52). On the whole, the impression that Willis leaves is that of a traveler comprehensively examining people who are, to his decidedly Western views, a benighted but curious object at best.

Even more instantaneously popular was John Lloyd Stephens' two-volume *Incidents of Travel in Egypt, Arabia Petraea, and the Holy Land*, which appeared in 1837, shortly after Willis' book. An immediate success, it was reprinted repeatedly "within little more than a year"[5] and was considered an authority on its subject. Stephens came to visit the Levant in a spirit of adventure, curious and perhaps fascinated by earlier accounts, but fundamentally concerned with the thrill of an exotic experience. As the preface indicates, he wanted "to give a narrative of the every-day incidents that occur to a traveler in the East, and to present to his country-men ... a picture of the widely different scenes" (I,v). Arriving at Alexandria in 1835, Stephens thence passed up the Nile as far as the Lower Cataracts. Returning from the Cataracts, he came to Cairo and then visited Mount Sinai and proceeded to the Holy Land. The book recounts Stephens' candid responses to the lands he visited and to the incidents that struck his mind. While they are essentially occupied with Stephens' journeying in Egypt and Arabia Petraea, and principally with his visit to the Holy Land, the two volumes also describe Arab manners, customs, and habits as they appeared to Stephens. Like Willis', Stephens' volumes contain unflattering generalizations or judgments about the Arab people he met. According to Stephens, "One who has never met an Arab in the desert can have no conception of his terrible appearance. The worst pictures of the Italian bandits or Greek mountain robbers I ever saw are tame in comparison" (I, 82). And, later in the narrative, he adds: "I had now been with them [the desert Arabs] ten days, and expected to be with them a month longer, to see them in their tents, and be thrown among different tribes ..., I was curious to know something of the lighter shades, the details of their lives and habits .... Wild and unsettled, robbers and plunderers as they are, they have laws which are as sacred as our own" (I, 204). He even shows mistrust in Arab punctuality. "The Arabs," says Stephens, "like most other Orientals, have no respect for the value of time; and among the petty vexations of traveling among them, few annoyed me more than the eternal 'bokhara,' 'bokhara,' 'to-morrow,' to-morrow'" (I, 140). Describing "a caravan of Mussulmans on their pilgrimage to Mecca," he writes: "They were a filthy set, many of them probably not changing their clothes from the time they left their homes until they had reached the tomb of the Prophet" (I, 188). Even though he had no real affection for the desert Arabs, Stephens was, in some ways, sympathetic to them. He writes: "I had still clung to the primitive simplicity and purity of the children of the desert, their temperance and abstinence, their contented poverty and contempt for luxuries as approaching the true nobility of man's nature, and sustaining the poetry of the 'land of the East.' But my last dream was broken; and I never saw among the wanderers of the desert any traits of character or any habits of life which did not make me prize and value more the privileges of civilization" (II, 124).

Fundamentally descriptive, Stephens' views of Arab life and beliefs were also analytical. In one such example, while he comments on the state of women among the Muslim Arabs, Stephens remarks:

> It is a vulgar prejudice, the belief that women are not admitted into the heaven of Muhammed. It is true that the cunning Prophet, in order not to disturb the joyful serenity with which his followers look forward to their promised heaven, has not given to women any fixed position there, and the pious Mussulman, although blessed with the lawful complement of four wives, is not bound to see among his seventy-two black-eyed houries the faces of his companions upon earth; but the women are not utterly cast out; they are deemed to have souls, and entitled to a heaven of their own; and it may be, too, that their visions of futurity are not less bright, for that there is a mystery to be unravelled beyond the grave, and they are not doomed to eternal companionship with their earthly lords. (I, 171)

Such an interpretation is distorted; for women are admitted into paradise in much the same way as men are. Nor are women entitled to a paradise of their own. But Stephens, as can be noted form the above passage, was overwhelmed by the experience of living among the Arabs so much that he was ready to give simplified interpretations of their Muslim beliefs and manners, among other things Islamic.

Fourteen years later, George William Curtis started his literary career with the publication of *Nile Notes of a Howadji* in 1851, which was followed by *The Howadji in Syria* the next year. The Howadji volumes were both based on his journey in 1849-1850 through the Levant. Well aware that there must be "a sympathy between the nature of the man and the country he visits,"[6] Curtis gave his books a subjective and impressionistic treatment. He organized his impressions loosely around the trip down the Nile and back in *Nile Notes*, and the journey from Cairo to Beirut in *The Howadji in Syria*. Curtis captured the atmosphere of the land through which he was traveling, and he infected his reader with his impressions. To be sure, Curtis viewed the Levant with the eyes of a poet, and his poetic impressions contain a profound sense of Levantine life and character. Early in *Nile Notes* Curtis points out that "if you would enjoy the land, you must be a poet, and not a philosopher.... The prominent interest is the picturesque one.... Be a pilgrim of beauty and not of morals or of politics, if you would realize your dream."[7] And he repeatedly emphasizes his point throughout the narrative. As he passed through Erment, a town on the Nile in Upper Egypt, Curtis was awakened by "a voluptuous morning.... Cloudless the sky ... warmly rosy the azure that domed the world .... The day itself was flower, and feast, and triumphal song. The day itself lingered luminously along the far mountain ranges, paling in brilliance, and over the golden green of the spacious plain, that was a flower-enameled pavement this morning, for our treading, as if unceasingly to remind us that we went as worshippers of beauty only, and the fame of beauty that fills the world" (*NN*, 265). Curtis considered himself a poet-traveler; and he endeavored to deal with the glamour of the Levant, both poetically and philosophically. "The Orient," writes Curtis, "is that primeval and perpetual noon. That very heat explains to you the voluptuous elaboration of its architecture, the brilliance of its costume, the picturesqueness of its life. But no Mozart was needed to show Persian gardens with roses breathing love and beauty, no Beethoven to build mighty Himalayas, no Rossini to sparkle and sing with the birds and streams. Those realities are there ... In the [Muslim] East, you fell and see music, but hear it never" (*NN*, 32).

To Curtis the East, "like the natures which it symbolizes," lives in extremes. "There is no measure, no moderation in its richness and beauty, or in its squalor and woe" (*NN*, 91). Curtis was in fact struck by an immeasurable contrast between the Oriental and American ways of life, and he was so profoundly aroused to life in the Levant that he exhorted the reader to discard "your hasty habits, and no longer bolt your pleasure as you do your Tremont or Astor dinner, but taste it all the way down, as our turbaned friends do" (*NN*, 37). While he describes the custom of "Salaaming," Curtis was amused to realize how much time the natives spend in greeting one another:

> It commences with touching hands and repeating some for-
> mula of thanks giving and prayer. It continues by touching
> hands and repeating the formula, which is by no means brief,
> and is rattled off as unconcernedly as Roman priests rattle off
> their morning masses, looking all around, and letting the
> words run. When it is finished, the parties kiss their own
> hands and separate. Generally, having nothing to say, they go
> apart after this elaborate greeting. (*NN*, 176)

Curtis' ardent love for the exotic, his interest in foreign scenery and landscape, and his devotion to the beauty of nature were characteristic traits in the Howadji volumes. He dwelt a great deal on the majesty of the Levant; the romantic scenery of the desert; the exotic charm of the Nile; and the cloudless skies. Several chapters were devoted to impressions of the sublimity of the Levantine highlands, to views of nature and of art. Such chapters as "The Landscape," "The Sun," "The Sakias," "Under the Palms," "A Crow That Flies in Heaven's Sweetest Air," "Ultima Thule," and "Sunset" in *Nile Notes* strike us as examples of Curtis' love for natural scenery and romantic expression. Curtis was interested in scenes essentially as mediums to induce colorful pictures of the sites and the people he saw.

An avowed "pilgrim of beauty", Curtis was among the very few American travelers who were attracted by "Oriental masculine beauty". And because he admired beauty, Curtis wanted to describe the people he met, especially those whom he considered as exemplars of the beautiful. He could see the beauty of the Orient in "the figures of men" he encountered while passing through the bazaar of the town of Asyut. "Oriental masculine beauty," says Curtis, "is so mild and feminine, that the men are like statues of men seen in the most mellowing and azure atmosphere. The forms of the face have a surprising grace and perfection. They are not statues of heroes and gods so seen ... ; the ripening, rounding lip, the arched brow, the heavy, drooping lid, the crushed, closed eye, like a bud bursting with voluptuous beauty, the low, broad brow; these I remember at Asyoot, and remember forever. There is nothing Western comparable with this .... Western beauty is intellectual, but intellectual has no share in this Oriental charm" (*NN*, 92). Similarly, Curtis was impressed by the complexion and the Bedouin features of Sheikh Artoosh (Curtis' guide during the journey to the river Jordan and the Dead Sea). To Curtis Artoosh was an ideal Bedouin who had "the arched brow, the large, rich, sad and tender eyes, which are peculiar to the Orient.... It was the most beautiful and luminous eye I have ever seen. The other features were delicate, but full of force, and the olive transparency of his complexion set his planet-like eyes, as evening light the stars. There was that extreme elegance in his face, and in the supple grace of his movement which imagination attributes to noblemen, and which is of the same quality as the refinement of a highbred Arabian horse" (*HIS*, 218). Obviously Curtis was captivated by the handsomeness of masculine features he observed in the Levant, features which he, as these passages suggest, found lacking in the West. Thus Curtis, rather rapturously perhaps, devotes entire chapters to the romance and beauty of the East as they appeared to him in the natives he came to encounter.

When he was in Esne, a town south of Luxor in Egypt, Curtis was captured by "fair frailty." He spent an evening in the bower of two dancing "ghawazee," and four chapters in *Nile Notes*, "Fair Frailty," "Fair Frailty- Continued," "Kushuk Arnem," and "Terpsichore," are devoted to this pleasurable experience. As he entered the bower, Curtis seated himself leisurely "upon the divan of honor." He tells us that "To sit, as Westerners sit, is impossible upon a divan. There is some mysterious necessity for crossing the legs" (*NN*, 131). "I seized the flowing tube of a brilliant amber-hued nargileh," says Curtis, "such as Hafiz might have smoked, and perhaps Isis that some stray Persian might chance along to complete our company" (*NN*, 132). The company was soon completed when "Kushuk Arnem entered her bower." Arnem was a young Egyptian, "a bud no longer, yet a flower not too fully blown" (*NN*, 132). The ghazeeyah addressed the Howadji in Arabic, when she came dancing in uttering "words whose honey they would not have distilled through interpretation" (*NN*, 133). There was something gay in the lady's figure. She had "large, laughing eyes, red, pulpy lips, white teeth, arching nose," and everything she wore attracted him.

Curtis, somewhat fancifully, details Arnem from top to bottom. Her feet were hid by "yellow Morocco slippers," over which "brooded a bewildering fullness of rainbow silk. Turkish trowsers we call them;" Curtis says, "but they are shintyan in Arabic" (*NN*, 134), and he goes on to say that "like the sleeve of a clergyman's gown, the lower end" of the trowsers was "gathered somewhere, and the fullness gracefully overfalls." Describing the ghazeeyah's upper half, he says: "A satin jacket, striped with velvet and of open sleeves, where from floated forth a fleecy cloud of undersleeve, rolling down the rosy arms, as June clouds down the western rosiness of the sky; inclosed the bust" (*NN*, 134). Her hair "much unctuated ... was adorned with a pendent fringe of black silk, tipped with gold, which hung upon the neck behind" (*NN*, 134). A bewildering, "dreamy vaprous veil" covered the upper part of her arms. But the veil concealed nothing of Arnem's beauty. Curtis could still see "beneath the tob, ... a beautiful bud-bursti-ness of bosom." Such an experience lent itself profoundly to Curtis' romantic imagination, stimulating all of his poetic sensations. He finally summed her up this way: "This brilliant cloud, whose spirit was Kushuk Arnem, our gay Ghazeeyah, gathered itself upon a divan, and inhaled vigorously a nargileh. A damsel in tob and Shintyan, exhaling azure clouds of aromatic smoke, had not been displeasing to that Persian poet, for whose coming I had prayed too late" (*NN*, 135). The romance of the Orient embodied in Kushuk Arnem and other natives Curtis came to know was more or less a medium for expressing poetic sensations or impressions about the Muslim Orient, impressions that are part of a traditional, preconceived picture which Curtis should have had in mind before he actually went to the region.

Occasionally, however, Curtis' views of the natives were judgmental. The national character of the Egyptians seemed to be influenced by the desert: "This fateful repose," explains Curtis, "this strange stillness, this universal melancholy in men's aspects, and in their voices, ... the intent but composed eagerness with which they listen to the wild romances of the desert, ... all this is of the desert" (*HIS*, 3-4). When he reached Jerusalem, Curtis was disappointed by its diminutiveness and smallness but especially by the friction between the various Christian sects who vied for preference in the Holy Land. With exasperation he says: "The Christians in Jerusalem are the worst of all Christians" (*HIS*, 192). "And here in Jerusalem," adds Curtis, "in the very presence of the Sepulchre, and the profound reality of Christ's life, ignorant and repulsive monks, quarrelling and dozing, and stambling in dirty gowns about a bare and desolate building, which looks like a dilapidated old curiosity shop, carrying disgusting idols through a crowd abjectly superstitious -- these things do not satisfy any known condition of delight" (*HIS*, 214). In no other place in the Howadji volumes does Curtis emphasize that he described exactly what he saw; that he spoke "merely of the fact, and strongly" (the fact that "the mass of Christians in Jerusalem have been the indelible stain upon the name they assume" [*HIS*, 215]). Such generalizations are relatively rare. And Curtis's main aim was to focus his accounts upon himself and upon his impressions as a traveler through the region. Since he generally showed a tolerant, sympathetic nature, the kind of impression which he leaves of the people and the lands he saw is by no means censorious, though it tends to be excessively romantic in some ways.

Curtis' contemporary, the thirty-year-old John Ross Browne, having visited Constantinople, arrived in Beirut in 1851, eager to visit the Holy Land. He soon hired Yusef Simon Badra, a Syrian dragoman to guide and protect him and Browne's two companions on an overland journey to Jerusalem by way of Damascus. Browne and his fellow travelers made their way across Lebanon, on to Damascus, and thence to Jerusalem by way of the Sea of Galilee and Nazareth. From Jerusalem they made a trek to the desert convent Mar Saba, the Dead Sea, the river Jordan, and Jericho. Later, Browne undertook a journey from Jerusalem to Bethlehem for the Christmas Eve ceremonies. Thence he returned to Jaffa, and traveled all the way north along the Mediterranean, passing through such seaports as Sidon and Tyre, back to Beirut again. Having completed his journey in the Holy Land in some forty days, Browne sailed for Egypt. And two years later, in 1853, he published *Yusef; or, the Journey of the Frangi: A Crusade in the East*, based on his experience as a traveler in the Levant.

Ross Browne entitled his book after his dragoman, Yusef, and, other than himself, he made him the principal character in the narrative. Like other characters in the book, Yusef was introduced with a pencil sketch that was accompanied with a lively verbal portrait: "Face open and intelligent, eyes round and full of fire, temperament nervous-sanguine, age twenty-eight, costume rich, careless, and dashing; figure well knit and of medium height; manner frank, self-relying, and chivalrous; whole tone of character imposing, captivating, and Oriental."[8] From the moment Yusef was hired as a dragoman in Beirut to the very end of the book, where he was behind prison bars, he played a significant role both through his dashing behavior and impetuous remarks, and Browne organized his book principally around Yusef's Arab features and views.

Let us see now how Yusef characterizes himself to the reader and to Browne, and how Browne in turn presents his Arab dragoman. Yusef's greatest distinctive feature was bravery. He assured Ross Browne that he was known throughout Syria as Badra the Destroyer of Robbers and that the last time he was out with a party of Frangis he had killed six Bedouins single-handedly (*Yusef*, 177). Yet he admitted only one fault--hatred of women--though he occasionally was on a quest for one or another of his pretty "nieces" who lived in almost every village they visited or passed through. Browne tells us that Yusef "never could refer to the subject [the female sex] without strong expressions of contempt and disdain. He considered that all the misfortunes of life could be traced to women; that the whole female sex consisted of devils in the disguise of angels" (*Yusef*, 180). Along the way Browne and Yusef dealt with such universal problems and truths as the proper treatment of women, the nature of human progress, and the secret of happiness. At times Browne placed much emphasis on Yusef's Arab views, and at other times emphasis was placed on Browne's own views of both American and Arab societies, quite often with a satirical touch. Thus Browne showed why

Americans gave their women liberty, while the Arabs kept theirs veiled and even enslaved.

> General. "It seems to me Yusef," said I, "that you Arabs are the most barbarous people on the face of the earth. Why even the Hottentots give their women some liberty. You, however, not only cover their faces, but keep them in a state of abject slavery. How can you ever expect to be a virtuous people when your wives are nothing but slaves!"
>
> Yusef (with spirit). "They are not such slaves as your excellency thinks. We shut them up and keep them at home when strangers are about ...; but, as a general thing, we treat them kindly...."
>
> General. ".... In America we never think of shutting our women up and keeping guard over them. They would soon mutiny against that."
>
> General (indignantly). "The bastinado, forsooth!.... No Yusef; we never use the bastinade...."
>
> General. "Tell me, Yusef, in the name of common sense ... what do Arab women cover their faces for?"
>
> Yusef. "Now, verily, O General, hast though asked me a question that it is difficult to answer. It is the custom of the country...."
>
> General. "But the custom is absurd, and ought to be abandoned at once."
>
> (*Yusef,* 227-228)

Browne eventually decides that "it was useless to argue with Yusef... ; that the Arabs were a very wicked and ignorant race at best, and he was more to blame for entertaining such monstrous doctrines, as he had enjoyed the advantages of intercourse with a more civilized people" (*Yusef,* 231). Browne's remarks about Arab women recall the long accepted tradition in the West that women are simply a veiled, suppressed element among Arabo-Islamic societies, and that they are always kept in a state of abject slavery. As the dialogue proceeds we realize that Yusef does not have much to say against such charges, finding it difficult to answer Browne's questions. Yet, for one reason or another, he remained content with the customs of his society which, to Browne's decidely Western views, can only be taken as "absurd."

Again, in a dialogue on the "Grand Secret of Human Happiness," which began with Browne's objections to the laziness of an Arab who spent most of the day smoking a narghile and most of the night sleeping, a contrast between Yusef's views of happiness, being "content with as little as possible," and Browne's support of industry and progress develops. The dialogue starts thus:

> General. "How is it, Yusef, that your countrymen never think of bettering their condition? See that lazy wretch basking in the sun there; why doesn't he go to work and do something useful? I verily believe he smokes all day and sleeps all night."
>
> Yusef. "And wherefore, O General, should he trouble his head about anything more? The very philosophy of life is to be content with as little as possible in this world."
>
> General. "Then he must be a great philosopher, for he certainly has no visible means of support. It takes uncommonly little to satisfy him, so far as I can see."
>
> Yusef. "Yet that little appears to be enough. He takes it easy, as you may perceive, and does not seem at all unhappy."
>
> General. "Faugh! What a barbarous life! A fine looking fellow like that fooling away his time basking in the sun like a great mud-turtle. Why, in our country he might earn his dollar a day."
>
> (*Yusef*, 285-286)

After a diversion on the similarity between Yusef's beatings of the muleteer and the flogging of seamen on American ships, the dialogue proceeds to a consideration of the virtues of industry that Yusef fell back on his enthusiasms for diversity: "That's the beauty of it--the very principle of existence! A Turk takes his ease in smoke; a Frenchman in dancing; a German in beer, talk, and pipes; and an Englishman in beef-steak; an American--pardon me, O General, I mean no disrespect in referring to your own words--an American in being uneasy. When he is uneasy he is easy, and when he is easy he is uneasy" (*Yusef*, 294). Acute as this remark may be, the confrontation between Browne's Western views and his Oriental dragoman's in such dialogues, though they may not be taken literally, amounts to a lightly prejudiced attitude towards the Muslim Orient on Browne's part. Browne's pro-Western preference for productivity and progress thus leads him to characterize the Orient as subordinate and even as "barbarous."

Browne disgraces Yusef in the end, Yusef's downfall came when, in the presence of a few attractive and admiring women, he had performed equestrain tricks, twirling the *djeered* above his head with which he once belabored Browne's weak, one-eye Arabian steed, shouting "Badra, Badra" as he clung to the steed's tail. Ironically enough, on this occasion, Yusef wanted to drop the *djeered* to the ground, only to find himself unable to get back into his saddle. He was even humiliated more when Mustapha, the muleteer, rescued him. And as the party finally returned to Beirut along the coast, Yusef's strength and bravery slowly declined. He made it clear to Browne that it hurt his conscience a great deal that he had killed no robbers during the trip, and when Browne threatened to have him in a book and tell the public about him, Yusef was encouraged to find at least one bad man to destroy. He immediately started to attack a camel driver, but he changed his mind and shook his hands instead. On the last day on the trip, Yusef, fortified with feelings of bravery, went ahead of the party, beat up a little Turk, pretending he was a giant Bedouin. But the little Turk went to the authorities to obtain justice and soon the Destroyer of Robbers was seized and put in Jail. "No more was he Yusef the brave!," writes Browne, "Yusef the Destroyer of Robbers! Throughout Beirut he was now, 'poor Yusef!' --nothing but 'poor Yusef!'" (*Yusef*, 419). When brave Yusef finally ends up in prison helpless as he is, he owes his appalling misfortune to woman, and he emphasizes further his bias against and repugnance to the female sex, which in turn Browne has endeavored to highlight and, in a way, ridicule in the course of the narrative. In fact, Browne in the end shows that his renowned dragoman was fierce and unrelenting in his prejudices, that the two ruling prejudices of his life were an intrinsic hostility to woman, and a voracious thirst for the blood of his fellow-creatures, and that it was Browne's constant task throughout the entire journey to restrain him from the indulgence of these unfortunate rather uncivilized propensities. Despising the whole female sex, as he did, Yusef thus declared that womankind was the root of all evil, and in the hope of overcoming these prejudices Browne, in a way that *seemed* to show aversion, deemed it his duty to afford all the counsel he had in his power to the unfortunate Yusef.

In the same year, 1851, Browne arrived in Beirut, Bayard Taylor was already aboard *Manchester City* bound for Liverpool, and thence to the Levant. Taylor's visit lasted ten months, two of which he spent in Nubia and the Sudan, regions never before visited by an American writer. His ten-month sojourn resulted in two travel narratives, *A Journey to Central Africa; or, Life and Landscapes from*

Egypt to the Negro Kingdoms of the White Nile and *The Lands of the Saracen;
or, Pictures of Palestine, Asia Minor, Sicily and Spain,* as well as a volume of
poetry, *Poems of the Orient,* all published in 1854. Another one-month visit to
Egypt in 1874 yielded *Egypt and Iceland.* Taylor went to the Levant to rest and
to recover his health. In the preface to *A Journey to Central Africa,* Taylor explained: "The Journey was undertaken solely for the purpose of restoring a frame
exhausted by severe mental labor. A previous experience of a tropical climate
convinced me that I should best accomplish my object by a visit to Egypt, and as
I had a whole winter before me, I determined to penetrate as far into the interior
of Africa as time would allow, attracted less by the historical and geographical
interest of those regions than by the desire to participate in their free, vigorous,
semibarbaric life."[9] But Traveling was also an education, a source of knowledge
and inspiration to satisfy Taylor's curiosity. He actually believed that "the first
end of travel is instruction, and that the traveler is fully justified in pursuing this
end, so long as he neither injures himself nor others" (*JCA*, 132). Recalling his
travel experience, some seventeen years after his visit to the Levant, Taylor writes: "I felt, it is true, that a visit to Greece, Egypt, and Syria was desirable in
order to complete my acquaintance with the lands richest in history of
civilization; and I would have been quite wiling to relinquish all chance of seeing
more of the world, had that much been assured to me."[10] With this in mind,
Taylor went to the Levant to acquaint himself with lands and people unknown to
him before and to tell the public about what he actually saw and felt.

Not long after his arrival in Egypt, Taylor observed that

> The best definition of an Arab which I can give is--a philoso-
> phizing sinner. His fatalism gives him a calm and equable
> temperament under all circumstances, and "God wills it!" or
> "God is merciful!" is the solace of every misfortune. But this
> same carelessness to the usual accidents of life extends also
> to his speech and his dealings with other men. I will not say
> that an Arab never speaks truth: on the contrary, he always
> does, if he happens to remember it, and there is no object to
> be gained by suppressing it; but rather than trouble himself to
> answer correctly a question which required some thought, he
> tells you whatever comes uppermost in his mind, though cer-
> tain to be detected the next minute. He is like a salesman,
> who, if he does not happen to have the article you want, of-
> fers you something else.... The people do not steal outright;
> but they have a thousand ways of doing it in an indirect and

111

civilized manner, and they are perfect masters of all those petty arts of fraud.

(*JCA*, 396-397)

In his definition of an Arab, Taylor, as the above passage reveals, emphasizes two points; first, the fatalism of an Arab; second, his fraud. Thus, while he alludes to the Arab's "carelessness to the usual accidents of life," Taylor points out that this carelessness in turn extends to "his speech" and to other affairs of his life, a carelessness which, if engaged in speech, makes him say whatever comes to his mind, ignoring perhaps the truth of what he communicates. Similarly, Taylor comments on other Arab manners, and he implicates them in "those petty arts of fraud." Taylor, I think, refers here to the habit of begging from travelers common at the time among the illiterate peasants (or *Fellahs*), and he shows his vulnerability to it, but he also shows, somewhat apologetically, that begging was conducted more or less in a "civilized manner." Yet, with these slight drawbacks, there is much to like in the Arabs. Taylor found that "the people of Egypt are fully as honest and well-disposed as the greater part of the Italian peasantry.... Their good humor," he wrote, "is inexhaustible. A single friendly word wins them, and even a little severity awakes no lasting feeling of revenge. I should much rather trust myself alone among Egyptian Fellahs, than among the peasants of the Campagna or the boors of Carinthia" (*JCA*, 102). The second visit to Egypt, in 1874, even enhanced his earlier "conclusion that there is no more cheerful and patient race in the world than the Egyptian Moslem [sic]. My remembrance of their nature, in this respect, is more than confirmed on seeing them again."[11]

Taylor thrilled at the experience of discovery and romance in Egypt and Nubia. "This was Central Africa as I had dreamed it," he wrote, "a great though savage picture, full of life and heat, and with a barbaric splendor even in the forms of Nature" (*JCA*, 328). The Nile in particular had much romantic appeal for him: "It had already become my home endeared to me not more by the grand associations of its eldest human history than by the rest and patience where I had breathed in its calm atmosphere" (*JCA*, 170). And in a poem, "To the Nile," he spoke of the river's ancient history and of its eternity thus:

Art thou the keeper of that eldest lore,
    Written ere yet thy hieroglyphs began,
When dawned upon thy fresh, untrampled shore
    The earliest life of Man?

Thou guardest temple and vast pyramid,

Where the gray past records its ancient speech;
    But in thine unrevealing breast lies hid
        What they refuse to teach.

All other streams with human joys and fears
    Run blended, o'er the plains of History:
Thou tak'st no note of man: a thousand years
        Are as a day to thee.[12]

As Taylor ventured into the interior of Africa, he was impressed further by the soothing, almost intoxicating atmosphere of the region. In another poem, "Nubia," the thrill of a glamorous, calm atmosphere is obvious.

A Land of Dreams and Sleep--a poppied land!
With skies of endless calm above her head,
The drowsy warmth of summer noonday shed
Upon her hills, and silence stern and grand
Throughout her desert's temple-burying sand.
Before her threshold, in their ancient place,
With closed lips, and fixed, majestic face
Noteless of Time, her dumb colossi stand.[13]

This is clearly a manifestation of Taylor's poetic sensations, a manifestation of the exotic romance and charm he beheld in the Muslim East.

    Taylor's second major Near-Eastern travel book, *The Lands of the Saracen,* containing his impressions about the Holy Land and Syria, including an account of his visits to Turkey, Sicily, and Spain. When he arrived in Jerusalem, Taylor soon "made the round of the Holy Sepulchre on Sunday, while the monks were celebrating the festival of the Invention of the Cross .... As the finding of the Cross by the Empress is almost the only authority for the places inclosed within the Holy Sepulchre, I went there inclined to doubt their authenticity, and came away with my doubt vastly strengthened. The building is a confused labyrinth of chapels, choirs, shrines, staircases, and vaults--without any definite plan or any architectural beauty...."[14] Not only did Taylor come to the conclusion that none of the localities in the Holy Sepulchre were authentic, but he in addition expressed even in greater detail his dismay at the practices of Christianity among the Christian communities in the Holy City. "Jerusalem is the last place in the world," writes Taylor,"where an intelligent heathen would be converted to Christianity. Were I cast here, ignorant of any religion, and were I to compare the lies and practices of different sects as the means of making my choice--in short, to judge of each faith by the conduct of its professors--I should at once turn Mussulman" (*LS*, 79). Thus, while he showed hard feelings toward the Christians in Jerusalem, he also showed admiration for the Muslims and interest in their religion. He even saw some affinity between Islam and his Quakerism: "The perfect simplicity and sincerity of Moslem [sic] worship appeals to the Quaker element of my own blood; so, when I enter a mosque, the signs of race and climate and the symbolism of faith fade away, and I only remember that we are fellow-believers in one God."[15] Even though in a way complimentary, Taylor's attitude toward Islam and the Muslims is contradictory. From time to time in the narrative, he exclaims, especially about certain sections in Syria: "What a paradise might be made of this country, were it in better hands!" (*LS*, 110). Or, more directly, "Give Palestine into Christian hands, and it will again flow with milk and honey" (*LS*, 52). And he says again "the Mosque--that blossom of Oriental architecture, with its crowning domes, like the inverted bells of the lotus, and its reed-like minarets, its fountains and marble courts--can only perish with the faith it typifies. I, for one, rejoice that, so long as the religion of Islam exists (and yet may its time be short), no Christian model can shape its house of worship" (*LS*, 345). So Taylor exhibited mixed, rather contradictory feelings towards the Muslim Orient, and while on the one hand he seems to have admired the simplicity and sincerity of the Muslims, he yet showed distrust in their faith on the other.

An accomplished writer as he was, Taylor, however, presented vividly the sensuous and exotic nature of the Levant in his travel narratives. In *The Lands of the Saracens*, he poses as both a foreign observer and occasionally as a participant in strange experiences. Such detailed descriptions of the luxury of the Turkish bath and of smoking the water pipe and drinking Turkish coffee, the chapters on the visions and ecstasies of the hasheesh, and on bathing and bodies not only show his involvement in the strange ways of different peoples, but in addition they build up an image of the voluptuousness and romance of the Orient as he saw it. The account of the pleasure and effects of the hasheesh is a revealing example. Taylor describes the thrills which ran through his nervous system as he took the intoxicating drug. A nervous thrill suddenly shot "throbbing along the nerves to the extremities of my body. The sense of limitation--of confinement of our senses within the bounds of our own flesh and blood--instantly fell away" (*LS*, 136). He lost sight of all idea of form, feeling that he "existed throughout a vast extent of space.... Within the concave that held my brain, were the fathomless deeps of blue; clouds floated there, and the winds of heaven rolled them together, and there shone the orb of the sun. It was--though I thought not of that at the time-- like a revelation of the mystery of omnipresence" (*LS*, 137). The effect receded. "Words cannot paint the overwhelming sense of the ludicrous which I then experienced. I writhed on my chair in an agony of laughter, which was only relieved by the vision melting away like a dissolving view; till, out of my confusion of indistinct images and fragments of images, another and more wonderful vision arose" (*LS*, 138). He continues: "Those finer senses, which occupy a middle ground between our animal and intellectual appetites, were suddenly developed to a pitch beyond what I had ever dreamed, and being thus at one and the same time gratified to the fullest extent of their preternatural capacity, the result was a single harmonious sensation, to describe which human language has no epithet. Mahomet's Paradise, with its palaces of ruby and emerald, its airs of musk and cassia, and its rivers colder than snow and sweeter than honey, would have been a poor and mean terminus for my arcade of rainbows. Yet in the character of this paradise, in the gorgeous fancies of Arabian Nights, in the glow and luxury of all Oriental Poetry, I now recognize more or less of the agency of hasheesh" (*LS*, 140). Such was the effect of the Oriental drug, intoxicating but gorgeous, so much so that "Mahomet's Paradise... would have been a poor and mean terminus for [Taylor's] arcade of rainbows." So Taylor enchantingly associated Muslim Paradise with a paradise of hashish as he was under the influence of the befuddling drug, and the result is an image of a sensuous paradise which is an illustration of his sensations as he recalled them. Such an illustration, however, reiterates the common simplification that, in Islam, the character of paradise could only be represented in terms of sensual gratification, ignoring thus its spiritual glow. Be this as it may, being a popular writer, Taylor was not only able to give his reader detailed descriptions of the culture and character of the regions he visited, but he also popularized the Muslim East. Even though he occasionally showed mistrust in Islam and the culture it embodied, he certainly carried no dislike for the Muslims and he enjoyed traveling in the Levant. But he showed a tendency to draw picturesque, often highly romantic, descriptions of what he observed and felt.

In 1846 John William De Forest, a twenty-four-year-old youth, sailed for Beirut to visit his brother, Dr. Henry De Forest, who was sent to the Levant in 1842 as a medical missionary. In search of health, John thought it was wise to travel, hoping that a change of climate would improve his condition (he suffered an attack of typhoid fever). From Beirut, De Forest made a number of visits to Jerusalem, Jaffa, Mount Lebanon, Damascus, and Baalbek. *Oriental Acquaintance; or, Letters from Syria*, published in 1856, was De Forest's first literary endeavor. Unlike most American travelers in the Levant, De Forest did not offer the reader much exciting action or adventure in *Oriental Acquaintance*, though he later wrote a romance, *Irene* (1879), that takes place near Mt.

Lebanon, and involves a conflict between Irene's choice among suitors and her duty as a missionary. In his travel narrative, he was content to write about forgotten and neglected ruins. In the letter entitled "Acquaintance in Ruins", De Forest says: "I shall continue silent concerning such widely famous places as Baalbec and Palmyra. But I recollect scores of lonely, forgotten old tombs, and temples, and cities, which absolutely seem to reproach me for not reminding the world of their hoary existence.... For the half-savages, who wander and abide under their shadow, understand not their broken teachings of history, and have no sympathy for their solemn passion of desolateness."[16] But his expectations and disappointments obtrude throughout the narrative. Soon after landing at Smyrna, De Forest writes: "Before reaching Turkey, my imagination was possessed by an idea which I knew to be absurd, but which I could not shake out of it. The fat Turk in the geography, and the wealth of the Arabian Nights, formed the warp and woof of my Eastern expectations. I fancied that each Oriental [Arab] possessed an independent fortune, and smoked interminable pipes, seated on luxurious cushions.... I was extremely shocked, therefore, to find the greatest part of the population at work..." (*OA*, 5). Though De Forest's "Eastern expectations" may be tolerant, they occasionally yielded unflattering generalizations about the peoples of the regions he visited. For instance, he expresses his dismay at "the numerous vices" of the Syrian society, especially lying. "This vice seems to be the most contemptible of all," writes De Forest, "because it is the most cowardly. A thoroughly brave boy tells the truth, no matter what are the jeers of his comrades, no matter what is the severity of the paternal rod. But the Syrians are morally neither brave boys nor brave men; and forever lie, on occasions ordinary and extraordinary" (*OA*, 230-231).

But like other travelers before him, De Forest was attracted to the *hareem* of the Orient, and we can see a single aspect of idealization. Following his landing in Beirut, the natives soon came to welcome him on his safe arrival. A young damsel caught his eye: "The girl's dark face, and excessively black hair and eyes, contrasted strongly with a gauzy white veil thrown over her head and falling down her shoulders. A dress fitting closely to the waist, and a shawl folded loosely round the hips, gave high relief to a slender, yet luxurious form, which stepped with a leisurely voluptuous motion. This southern ease and voluptuousness seemed to be her natural character" (*OA*, 39). Voluptuousness and gorgeousness were also remarkable features of another lady, Aseen of the Bait Susa, who came to see De Forest. She "advanced with the slow, voluptuous tread of her country-women, murmuring all the while smiling salutations in hyperbolical Arabic. Some fragments of her conversation were translated to me, but they have blown away, as lightly as thistle downs, from my memory. She bowed her head to let me examine its golden adornments. Perhaps she flattered herself at the impression such splender must produce on the youthful Howadji from the New World. She had better have rejoiced in her blue eyes and fair cheeks; for it was they principally that fixed my wonder" (*OA*, 42). Such detailed descriptions of the magnificent appearance of Middle Eastern women seem to be not only romantic, but also highly idealized, and it is only on this subject that he deviates from his generally reductionist attitude toward the Muslim Orient.

De Forest's romantic imagination was captivated by the superstitions that he often reports. In one such example De Forest tells us about a certain old Abdullah who came upon a house demanding some money. The lady of the house denied that she had any. But when Abdullah marched through the house "with a look of intense admiration," the lady gave him a little money, and bade him to depart at once. De Forest explains: "She [the lady] believed in the *evil eyes*. Many Syrians dislike to hear unmixed praise bestowed upon a child or a favorite horse or house, lest envy should be excited, and somebody's malignant optics should smite the coveted possession with a curse. Often a few beads are put round the neck of a boy or pretty girl, or a fine horse, or an egg is suspended in the arched doorway of a new house, or a defect is purposely left in a splendid room, in order to attract attention of gazers, and ward off the evil influence" (*OA*, 64-65). Such superstitious beliefs might have been accepted among some illiterate peasants, and De Forest, in a way that showed much romance, elaborated these beliefs. Another superstition that captured De Forest's attention was the "strange" names Arab parents give to their children. Parents who suffer the loss of a child or more name subsequent children after wild beasts to ward off evil influences. "They imagine often that such deaths came to them through some secret and malignant influence. Therefore, to break the fatal charm, they name the next child after some ferocious wild beast. Thus, Deebs and Nimmers, that is wolves and tigers, are quite plentiful...; and if you meet an individual with such a name, you may know, without asking, that he has some elder brother in the grave" (*OA*, 229-230). Though the one-year residence in Syria actually allowed De Forest to observe closely Arab society -Arab manners, customs, mores, superstitions, and beliefs- it did not seem to afford him much opportunity to penetrate further the culture and people of the region, but it certainly enabled him to romanticize the Muslim Orient.

Among major nineteenth-century American writers Mark Twain, in *The Innocents Abroad; or, the New Pilgrim's Progress*, published in 1869, well after the first flurry of travel books on the Levant, and Herman Melville, in *Clarel: A Poem and Pilgrimage in the Holy Land* (1876), make major use of the Muslim Near Orient. While Mark Twain's book is a classic of native American humor,

117

Herman Melville's poem is deeply serious and especially interesting in its philosophical use of the setting he observed on a trip to Palestine (1857). In this extraordinarily long narrative-poem of travel and philosophical argument, young Clarel, an American divinity student visiting Palestine, falls in love with a lovely converted Jewess, Ruth. Because, after her father's death, Clarel is forbidden by religious custom to visit her for a time, he sets off on a pilgrimage to the shrines of the Holy Land. Falling in with a group of other pilgrims (all presumably seeking evidence of religious truth), he undertakes a pilgrimage that takes him to the Jordan, the Dead Sea, the Greek monastery of Mar Saba in the mountains, then Bethlehem. The pilgrims embody various creeds and attitudes--Derwent, Church of England liberalism; Ungar, Roman Catholicism of the American South; Margoth, science; Nehemiah, blind faith; Vine, uncommitted and reserved individualism; Mortmain, misanthropy; Rolf, naturalistic skepticism. Most of the discussions and arguments revolve around such topics as paganism versus Christianity, Roman Catholicism versus Protestantism and modernism, science versus religion, and the like. On his return to Jerusalem at the end Clarel, however, finds that Ruth has died of grief in his absence, and his future becomes more uncertain than ever.

To be sure, young Clarel comes to the Muslim Near Orient motivated mainly by religious curiosity, by a desire to see the Holy Land -- the old land of prophetic revelations. We first see Clarel alone in his chamber on his first evening in Jerusalem.

> The dust lies, and on him as well--
> The dust of travel. But anon
> His face he lifts--in feature fine,
> Yet pale, and all but feminine
> But for the eye and serious brow--
> Then rises, paces to and fro,
> And pauses, saying, "other cheer
> Than that anticipated here,
> By me the learner, now I find."
> (I, 1, 3)[17]

As thoughtful and profound as Clarel's expectations of the Muslim Near Orient may be, they are, in fact, part of the deluding effect of books, and Clarel now realizes that books were no sufficient source for actual knowledge of the region he is traveling in.

"Needs be my soul,
Purged by the desert's subtle air
From bookish vapors, now is heir
To nature's influx of control...;
But here unlearning, how to me
Opens the expanse of time's vast Sea!
Yes, I am young, but Asia old.
The books, the books not all have told."
                    (I, 1, 5)

The Orient that we see in *Clarel* is, then, a different Orient altogether; it is one that has none of the glamor, the exoticism, and peculiarities, with the exception of a spiritual atmosphere, it is expected to have. And Clarel blames his "unlearning" on books: "the books not all have told."[18]

But *The Innocents Abroad* was no *Clarel*, and Mark Twain's book was more travel-oriented than Melville's poem. In the summer of 1867 Mark Twain made his trip to the Levant as a correspondent for the West's most prominent daily, the *San Francisco Alta California*. Arriving in Beirut, after having visited Turkey and other Levantine regions, Mark Twain, with seven companions accompanied by a dragoman and muleteers, set out to Jerusalem by way of Damascus, and he covered in three weeks the same itinerary that Browne had followed during his forty-day journey, with the exception that Mark Twain rejoined the *Quaker City* at Jaffa and thence he proceeded to Egypt aboard her, rather than returning to Beirut as Browne had done. But the sixteen years that had elapsed between the two journeys had brought a considerable change to the Levant; besides Mark Twain was more of a "tourist" doing a job, than a mere pilgrim or traveler. Mark Twain made the most of his travel experiences in the Levant. His newspaper letters in the *Alta California*, supplemented by the few he had written for the *New York Tribune*, with some minor revisions, were all included in the two-volume *The Innocents Abroad*. I will focus attention specifically on Mark Twain's recorded experiences as a traveler in Morocco, Turkey, and the Holy Land, which are only part of his travels in this book.

When he arrived in Tangier, Morocco, Mark Twain was immediately struck with the quality of "foreignness" of the city, and fanciful expectations are emphasized at the outset. "We wanted something thoroughly and uncomprisingly foreign--," writes Mark Twain, "foreign from top to bottom-foreign from center to circumference-- foreign inside and outside and all around-- ... nothing to remind us of any other people or any other land under the sun. And lo! in Tangier we have found it."[20] The emphasis on foreignness continues, and he proceeds with a catalogue of the people: "There are stalwart Bedouins..., and stately Moors... and Jews...; and swarthy Riffians..., and original, genuine Negroes as black as Moses; and howling dervishes and a hundred breeds of Arabs--all sorts and descriptions of people that are foreign and curious to look upon" (I, 65). This is a depiction of a typically alien society, and Mark Twain, in a way that never fails to show a sense of humor on his part, tells more about this society: "The people of Tangier (Called Tingis, then) lived in the rudest possible huts, and dressed in skins and carried clubs, *and were as savage as the wild beasts* [italics mine] they were constantly obliged to war with" (I, 68). He proceeds to depict the market-place, comparing the "civilized" with the uncivilized. "The general size of a store in Tangier," says Mark Twain, "is about that of an ordinary shower-bath in a civilized land. The Mahommedan merchant, tinman, shoemaker, or vender of trifles sits cross-legged on the floor, and reaches after any article you may want to buy. You can rent a whole block of these pigeonholes for fifty dollars a month. The market-people crowd the market-place with their baskets of figs, dates, melons, apricots, etc., and among them file trains of laden asses, not much larger, if any, than a Newfoundland dog. The scene is lively, is picturesque, and smells like a police court" (I, 69).

Nor did Turkey make a better impression. Mark Twain viewed Abdul Aziz, the Sultan of Ottoman Turkey, as "the representative of a people by nature and training filthy, brutish, ignorant, unprogressive, superstitious" (I, 120). Abdul Aziz is "weak, stupid, ignorant," Mark Twain adds, "almost as his meanest slave; chief of a vast royalty, yet the puppet of his premier and the obedient child of a tyrannial mother; a man sits upon a throne ... yet who sleeps, sleeps, eats, eats, idles with his eight hundred concubines [i.e., wives], and when he is surfeited with eating and sleeping and idling, he would rouse up and take the reins of government and threaten to *be* a Sultan" (I, 121-122). The Sultan had denied the freedom of the press in Turkey; for Mark Twain this was an unparadonable sin, and so he stereotyped him as some kind of dull beast. Mark Twain's response to the Turkish culture was wholly negative. Turkey was, for Mark Twain, a nation of oppressed beggars: "If you would see the very heart and home of cripples and human monsters both, go straight to Constantinople. A beggar in Naples who can show a foot which has all run into one horrible toe, with one shapeless nail on it, has a fortune--but such an exhibition as that would not provoke any notice in Constantinople" (II, 69). Increasingly, however, the dirt and the wretchedness of the Turks and everything Turkish--Turkish baths, Turkish food, Turkish coffee, Turkish tobacco--become a joke and a source of humor.

When Mark Twain began his inland excursion into Lebanon, Syria, and Palestine, he again sympathized and empathized with the Arab natives. The "people are naturally good-hearted," writes Mark Twain, "and intelligent, and, with education and liberty, would be a happy and contented race" (II, 165). As he moved farther into Syria, he became more and more distressed over the conditions of the natives. He pronounced the Damascenes to be "the ugliest, wickedest-looking villains we have seen" (II, 183). Much emphasis is placed on the filthiness and misery both of the land and its people. Mark Twain writes:

> A Syrian village is a hive of huts one story high (the height of a man), and as square as a dry-goods box; it is mudplaster all over, flat roof and all, and generally white-washed after a fashion. The same roof often extends over half the town, covering many of the streets, which are generally about a yard wide. When you ride through one of these villages at noonday, you first meet a melancholy dog, that looks up at you and silently begs that you won't run over him, but he does not offer to get out of the way; next you meet a young boy without any clothes on, and he holds out his hand and says "Bucksheesh!" --he don't really expect a cent, but then he learned to say that before he learned to say mother, and now he cannot break himself of it; next you meet a woman with a black veil drawn closely over her face, and her bust exposed; finally, you come to several sore-eye children and children in all stages of mutilation and decay; and sitting humbly in the dust, and all fringed with filthy rags, is a poor devil whose arms and legs are gnarled and twisted like gra-pevines. These are all the people you are likely to see. The balance of the population are asleep within doors, or abroad tending goats in the plains and on the hill sides.... A Syrian village is the sorriest sight in the world, and its surroundings are eminently in keeping with it.
> (II, 192-193)

The closer Mark Twain comes to examining the natives, the more hopeless his verdicts seem to be. He spends pages describing the village of Magdala, and especially the "stupid population ... the blind, the crazy, and the cripple, all in ragged, soiled, and scanty raiment, and all abject beggars by nature, instinct, and education" (II, 234). Mark Twain described the people he met throughout Syria. He depicts the usual assemblage in a Syrian village this way: "They reminded me much of Indians, did these people. They sat in silence and with tireless patience watched our every motion .... They were infested with vermin and the dirt had

121

caked on them till it amounted to bark .... The children were in a pitiable condition--they all had sore eyes and were otherwise afflicted in various ways" (II, 199). And when he reaches the village of Ednor, his description becomes even harsher: "They were the wildest hordes of half-naked savages we have found thus far. They swarmed out of mud bee-hives .... It was Magdala over again, only here the glare from the infidel eyes was fierce and full of hate .... Dirt, degradation, and savagery are Ednor's speciality" (II, 276-277).

As Mark Twain walked in the dust and heat of Palestine, where Jesus of Nazareth once trod, and confronted directly his questioning of the authenticity of Biblical accounts, the filth and dirt of the populace, the evidences of sectarian bickering even in the holiest of all Christian shrines, all these corroborated his skepticism and challenged his belief in a God whose ethic he nevertheless deeply respected. Mark Twain's portrayal of the modern descendants of Biblical Palestine may be in part a reflection of his feelings as he wrestled with his religious beliefs and doubts.

> Christ knew how to preach to these simple, superstitious, disease-tortured creatures: He healed the sick. They flocked to our poor human doctor this morning when the fame of what he had done to the sick child went abroad in the land, and they worshipped him with their eyes while they did not know as yet whether there was virtue in his simples or not. The ancestors of these--people precisely like them in color dress, manners, customs, simplicity--flocked in vast multitudes after Christ, and when they saw Him make the afflicted whole with a word, it is no wonder they worshipped Him. No wonder His deeds were the talk of the nation. No that at one time--thirty miles from here--they had to let a sick man down through the roof because no approach could be made to the door; no wonder His audiences were so great at Galilee that he had to preach from a ship removed a little distance from the shore; no wonder that even in the desert places about Bethsaida, five thousand invaded His solitude, and he had to feed them by a miracle or else see them suffer for their confiding faith and devotion; no wonder when there was a great commotion in a city in those days, one neighbor explained it to another in words to his effect: "They say that Jesus of Nazareth is come!"
>
> (II, 201)

Mark Twain's final verdict is: "Palestine is desolate and unlovely." But it remains "sacred to poetry and tradition" (II, 359). By and large, Mark Twain's almost uniform views of Near Eastern peoples are a little bit curious. He does not seem to have found one native who actually penetrated beyond his senses, or to whom He warmed and attempted to look upon with the reputed Mark Twain affection. He obviously found no nigger Jim among the Near Eastern populace. And he does not seem to have seen in these people qualities of affection and kindness. Thus Mark Twain has focused attention throughout *The Innocents Abroad* on the foreignness, filthiness, and misery both of the Levant and its people, and has given in turn humorous but exaggerated portraits the American reader cannot but laugh at.

Despite the thrilling romanticism of Willis, Curtis, and Taylor, which was afterall real enthusiasm for the exotic nature of the Muslim Near Orient, the humor of Browne, the allegory of Melville, and the satire of innocent American tourists of Mark Twain, few of the travel accounts acquainted the reader with real Arab, and thus Muslim, manners; the chief reason being that the travelers did not themselves know the Arabs closely. And the fact that they had no actual knowledge both of the people they encountered and monitored and the region they traveled in made it even easier for them to form stereotypes and more or less preconceived images of the extrinsic nature of the Muslim Orient. Not being serious examiners of the culture or the people but travelers, they did not venture very far in exploring the inner society, nor did they intimately immerse themselves in the ways of the people they came to know to arrive at a more tolerant understanding, and to create a more accurate, more sympathetic image of them.

Notes

1 See, for a very useful overview, James A. Field's *America and the Mediterranean World, 1776-1882* (Princeton: Princeton University Press, 1969). The book traces the American activities in the Muslim Near East throughout the nineteenth century. Also helpful is A.L. Tibawi's *American Interests in Syria, 1800-1901* (London: Oxford University Press, 1966). Tibawi examines in depth the American educational, literary, and religious activities in Syria. And David H. Finnie's *Pioneers East* (Cambridge: Harvard University Press, 1967) has an eight-page appendix which lists American writing relating to American activities in the Near East before 1850.

2 Ahmed M. Metwali, "Americans Abroad: The Popular Art of Travel Writing in the Nineteenth Century," in *America: Exploration and Travel*, ed. Steven E. Kagle (Bowling Green, Ohio: Bowling Green State University Press, 1979), p. 68.

3 Maxime Rodinson, "The Western Image and Western Studies of Islam," in *The Legacy of Islam*, 2nd ed. ed. Joseph Schacht (London: Oxford University Press, 1974), p. 48.

4 *Pencillings by the Way*, 2 Vols. (Philadelphia: Carey, Lea, and Blanchard, 1836), II, 120-121. All subsequent references hereon refer to this edition. Page and volume numbers are in the text.

5 *Incidents of Travel*, 11th ed. (New York: Harper and Brothers, 1867), I, iii. Hereafter page and volume numbers from this edition are in the text.

6 *The Howadji in Syria* (New York: Harper and Brothers, 1877), p. 86. Other references in the text follow this edition.

7 *Nile Notes of a Howadji* (New York: Harper and Brothers, 1856). Subsequent references hereon follow this edition.

8 *Yusef; or, the Journey of the Frangi* (New York: Harper and Brothers, 1853), p. 178. I shall be using this edition throughout.

9 *A Journey to Central Africa* (New York: G.P. Putnam's Sons, 1875), p. 2. Hereafter page reference from this edition is in the text.

10 *By Ways of Europe* (New York: G.P. Putnam's Sons, 1891), p. 9.

11 *Egypt and Iceland* (New York: G.P. Putnam's Sons, 1870), p. 40.

12 *Poems of the Orient* (Boston: Ticknor and Fields, 1854), pp. 111-112.

13 *Ibid.*, p. 97.

14 *The Lands of the Saracen* (New York: G.P. Putnam's Sons, 1882), p. 82.

15 *Egypt and Iceland*, p. 42.

16 *Oriental Acquaintance* (New York: Dix, Edwards and Co., 1856), p. 267. Other references hereon refer to this edition.

17 Quotations in the text follow *Clarel: A Poem and Pilgrimage in the Holy Land*, ed. Walter E. Bezanson (New York: Hendricks House, 1960).

18 Dorothee Metlitsky Finkelstein has examined Herman Melville's use of, and concern with, the Orient in *Melville's Orienda* (New Haven: Yale University, 1961). The book shows the depth and extent of Melville's interest in the Near Orient, and how it affected his work.

19 For a very useful analysis of Mark Twain's experience as a traveler in the Levant, see Franklin Walker's *Irreverent Pilgrims* (Seattle: University of Washington Press, 1974), pp. 194-224; and, for a more stimulating review, Deway Ganzel's *Mark Twain Abroad* (Chicago: University of Chicago Press, 1968). Also helpful is Richard F. Fleck's essay "The Complexities of Mark Twain's Near Eastern Stereotyping," *Mark Twain Journal* 21 (1982): 13-15.

20 *The Innocents Abroad*, 2 vols. (New York: Harper and Brothers, 1911), I, 64. Henceforth volume and page numbers from this edition are in the text.

Chapter Five :

Finale

The American literary and cultural "awareness" of the Muslim Orient (or the Near East as some prefer to say) was largely an enterprise based on indirect encounter, and especially for nineteenth-century Americans the meeting of a New World and glamorous, romantic East was essentially an exotic experience. It is true that a handful of travelers had some opportunity of observing directly and that religious missionaries had more extended contact with the Muslims (Arabs, Turks, Persians, etc.), but many authors who dealt with, wrote about, or availed themselves of the idea of a Muslim East were forced to rely on the printed page -- books and other sources written by students who had no real opportunity to investigate and to *know* the Orient at first hand. European writers, the British romanticists in particular, played a tremendous role in the formation of the American reception of Muslim thought and character. Indeed, for obvious links of culture, much of the history of the American awareness of Oriental themes and ideas may be explained as an integral part of the European, especially the British, discovery of the Muslim East. European misconceptions of Islam and the Muslims were certainly at the root of the early American misconception, just as more accurate representations followed improvement in European knowledge. So the problem was partly fragmentary sources and faulty knowledge, but the root cause was the deeply established Occidental preconception.

My investigation throughout this work has sought to trace the American literary representations, and naturally the misrepresentations, of the Muslim Orient, but, in fact, most of the treatment has been focused on Washington Irving, Ralph Waldo Emerson, John Greenleaf Whittier, and the travelers as a group. Irving's interest in Islam, conspicuous in such works as *The Conquest of Granada, The Alhambra,* and *Mahomet and His Successors*, is natural in view of his preoccupation with Muslim Spain. But his presentation of the material is purely in the romantic tradition. The emphasis is on the Moorish King Boabdil El Chico and his hopeless struggle to regain the kingdom of Granada, and the legends of *The Alhambra* have the familiar features of the *Arabian Nights*. Finally, *Mahomet and His Successors* is the picturesque biography of the Prophet as a hero of Arabian romance rather than adequate account of his life. Emerson, on the other hand, found a strong affinity between Oriental thought -- Muslim and otherwise -- and his own. He showed genuine admiration for the Sufi poets of Persia; he referred to, and quoted, them extensively both in his prose as well as in his poetry. But, in spite of his enthusiasm for the Orient, Emerson was proud of his Western heritage, and he believed in the superiority of the West. Contemporary with Emerson, Whittier, a conservative moralist who was by no means interested in Muslim culture or literature, illustrated yet another use of Islam in connection with his moral war against the evils of human society and especially slavery, and he complemented the image of the period. Americans eventually went to the Muslim East, motivated mainly by strong desires to see the Holy Land -- the land of the three religions of the world -- but chiefly by a feeling for the foreign, the bizarre, and the exotic. The travelers actually saw the Muslim Near Orient, and what they saw was a preconceived picture which had long persisted in their imagination. In their accounts, the emphasis was on the romance and glamour of the East, but it also was on the wretchedness of the people they came to see.

Nineteenth-century American representations of an idea of the Muslim Orient have continuities and reiterations well into the recent past, and distorted perceptions have survived in the back of the American mind only to be summoned from a dead past into a recent one. Kenneth Roberts, in *Lydia Bairey* (1947), describes the conflict with the Barbary Pirates (1801-1805). Roberts recalls several years of the United States history, and the novel, though essentially a romance, shows the narrator's involvement in the Barbary war. The narrator, Albion Hamlin, thinks he is in love with a certain Harriet Faulkner, but he can never forget attractive Lydia Bailey, whom he saw only in a portrait. When he happens to learn that she is alive, Albion immediately dismisses Harriet from his thought and hurries to Haiti. Here he finds Lydia, and becomes acquainted with the influential King Dick, a Negro general who fought against the French. After Lydia and Albion marry, they plan to go to France, and then to visit King Dick's home in North Africa, only to be taken captives by the Barbary Pirates. In Tripoli, Lydia becomes governess for the three children of Hamet Karamanli, exiled brother of the ruling Pasha, Yusuf Maramanli. Meanwhile, Albion cultivates the gardens of Murad Rais, a Scotchman acting as admiral for Tripoli. For two years, Lydia secretly sends Albion letters describing how the Pasha demands payments from the United States in return for protection for American ships. Since the United States Navy is cruising in the Mediterranean, Albion cannot understand their failure to "knock that castle of Joseph Karamanli into a cocked hat,"[1] and he can do nothing but ponder his experience as a captive. As he comes to "know" more about Tripoli, Albion learns that

> Arabs have been taught by Mohammed that they are better than any other people ... ; that Arabs are the greatest liars in the world; that ... [they are] as ignorant as they are bigoted; and their word for God is always on the Arab's lips, to such a degree that hundreds of them often sway their bodies to and fro and cry out "Allah!" for hours on end; that the phrase *Bism' Allah* -- in the name of God -- accompanies every Arab's every action, no matter how absurd, trifling, childish, or evil: he says *Bism' Allah* when he ... kicks his donkey, when he slaps his wife's face, when he steals from a fellow traveler, when he cuts his father's throat, when he curses, ... when he spits upon an American captive ....
> (pp. 340-341)

Even though he could not go into Tripoli himself, through Lydia's letters, Albion came to know it as well as though he had lived there all his life. Lydia told him of the customs, the manners, the prayers, and the beliefs of the Arabs, and the little things he was not able to see himself. But the things she wrote him about were more or less a caricature; she told him that the Arabs were peculiar but weird people, and as such Albion accepted them. However, after two years of captivity, Albion, together with Lydia Bailey, escapes returning to France. But he has learned a lesson, as General Eaton, the American Consul at Tunis, has already done. "One thing I have learned in the three years I have been in North Africa," says Eaton, "is that there is nowhere an American can get worse treatment than in Moslem countries" (p. 407), and captivity experience causes Albion to be more acutely aware of the national integrity of the United States: "Joseph Karamanli had insulted America and declared war on her, which was something that Americans could never forgive" (p. 370-371).

Not very long ago, however, Laurie Devine in a historical, if somewhat socio-political, romance, *The Nile* (1983), captured the saga of two misfortunate lovers who meet and fall into an impossible love relationship until war and religion tear their world, and eventually their own beings, apart, and the novel revolves around the contemporary Egyptian and "Israeli" history from the end of World War II to the Camp David Accords. *The Nile* opens on a weird scene in a small Egyptian village, Kom Ombo, where life, according to Devine, has virtually remained the same since the days of the Pharaohs. It is a world of awkwardness, peril, and jeopardy. On the day when a pitiless, if not brutal, ritual marks young Mona's coming of age, the girl's mother asserts that "some sort of *tahara* (i.e., circumcision) was necessary ... to be protected against the dangers of her own wild sexual nature," and that such a ruthless rite was for her daughter's "own good" (p. 21).[2] In almost much the same way the father remarks: "It is the custom. It will make her clean" (p. 11). When what was left between Mona's legs was "a chastity belt of blood, skin, and shame" (p. 17). Meanwhile, Youssef al - Masri, Mona's lover and unwedded husband, is growing up in an invincible, affluent, temporal Jewish family in the upper-class Westernized world of Alexandria, and he is, the narrator tells us, "the very picture of sophistication" (p. 34). In Mona's eyes, Youssef was even "the prince of [his] family. He looked like a fairy-tale prince, with that mane of tousled blond hair, those even features, and that lordly carriage. He acted like a prince .... [He] was a golden boy, one of the lucky ones born with good looks, money, and a nature so easy going no one could hold any of it against him" (pp. 58-59). Whether what the village-girl sees in her charming boy turns out to be true or not is none of our concern at this point, but it is germane to our purpose to indicate that the al-Masris led a sleek life, and that Youssef was foreordained at best for a promising life at the powerful center of Alexandria's cosmopolitan set, and at worst for a purposeless life of belly-dancer, hashish-oriented debauchery until the emergence of Mona at the Villa al-Masri as a maid-servant, innocent, immature, and unsophisticated as she was, and he in turn "made even Mona seem a princess" (p. 98). Soon after her arrival at the al-Masris', a six-year old Mona attracts tall-fair-haired Youssef, yet light years away she becomes the boy's fantasy, and casual interest in Mona develops into flamboyant love so much so that she was "the most beautiful girl he had ever seen" (p. 152). "Youssef had thought of Mona often," the narrator tells us, "usually when he was ... lying in his bed. But sometimes she would come to his mind when he was in the midst of a conversation, and a slight smile would play on his lips." Expectedly, Mona too was falling in love with Youssef: "She magnified the significance of Youssef's every word and basked in the memory of his every smile. That look, those smiles, were her morning tea and bread, her dinner meat and rice, her supper eggs and toast. All day she longed for night so she could go to bed and give herself over to dreams of Youssef" (p. 155). Such was the kind of love that the two initiates came to feel. It is no surprise, therefore, that Youssef expected Mona to be his wife somehow, and that Mona always desired that she would. Thus it would not be too long before Mona became the princess of Villa al-Masri, for Youssef and she, they both hope, would live happily ever after, as Mona herself since her first appearance at the Villa dreamed would be their destiny.

As the narrator puts it, "it was Western, it was European, it was Enlightened, to believe that all things were possible for a man of goodwill. Putting it even more boldly, it was Eastern, it was Islamic, it was bitterly but deliciously mystical to have a sight and simply accept whatever calamaties came" (p. 163). Such a claim gives the Eastern, or the Islamic, a space where it stands vis-à-vis the European, that is, "The Enlightened," where certain boundaries and categories are set up, associations and distinctions made. The West, as the quotation obviously highlights, is associated here with enlightenment and wisdom, and this distinction suppresses the Muslim Orient to a substructural level that is characterized by passivity and resignation. Thus while the narrator leaves with the Western accuracy and intelligence, she leaves unimplorable fate with the Eastern. As we can see, East and West are culturally defined at this point. The difference between them is not geographical, nor is it racial; it is only a difference in the cultures that distinguish the two worlds. In any case, Devine's Western prejudice is too evident to be missed: she implies the inert in characterizing the Muslim Orient, but emphasizes "the Enlightened in characterizing the Western heritage which clearly stands higher. In fact the problems that we encounter in the novel, emotional, political, and otherwise, the poverty, the disease, the lack of progress, and fate, are blamed on Islam, and towards the end of the narrative once again we are reminded that "the fatalism of Islam might have allowed [the Muslims] to accept the random blows of their lives without going mad," and Youssef wonders: "but had not it also kept them from trying to make their lives better?" (p. 461). Whether we agree or not, naive Mona was highly convinced that whatever was to happen between her and her lover would happen. Now that she was pregnant, she was not quite certain what she was going to be able to do with Youssef being aware that marriage between a Jew and a Muslim is at best most unusual, but she thought that such a marriage was always conceivable, even when she discovered that Youssef, now a soldier in "Israel," married an Israeli girl and had three daughters, and that he may never come back again to her. But after all, who was she to question the will of *Allah*? There was no turning back. May be she had never had much choice in this matter anyway. At any rate, Muslim Mona never married Jewish Youssef. Helpless as she was, Mona prayed for forgiveness, she prayed for guidance, she prayed for the strength to endure what, it seemed, *Allah* had ordained for her, and all she was able to do at the end was to surrender to a most cheerless and sorrowful fate.

A year later, Leon Uris in a picaresque, historical novel, *The Haj* (1984), traced the Arab-Israeli conflict between 1929 and 1956. The hero of the novel, a Palestinian Arab, Haj Ibrahim al Soukri al Wahabi, Mukhtar (or head) of Tabah, is forced to leave his village in the vortex of the struggle for Palestine. In the novel, Haj Ibrahim is introduced through a dual narrative recited, on the one hand, in the first-person voice of his young son, Ishmael, and, on the other hand, in the voice of an omniscient narrator that presumably speaks for the author himself. What is remarkable throughout the book is a sternly unflattering image of the Muslim Arabs in general and the Palestinian Ibrahim in particular. Page after page, the Arabs, the Haj included, are presented as inhuman, cowardly, lustful and hateful, and hatred becomes the novel's major theme. In one such example, Dr. Nuri Mudhil, in a way that edges into autoaccusation, tells Ishmael: "Islam is unable to live at peace with anyone. We Arabs are the worst .... We have contributed nothing to human betterment in centuries, unless you consider the assassin and the terrorist as human gifts."[3] Young Ishmael does not have much to argue against Mudhil's views since he himself believes that the Arabs are indeed "the worst." Why Ishmael shows abhorence of his own race is not justified. What is clear is that he has dismal feelings for his ruthless father, and these may in part explain why he in the end becomes content with what Dr. Mudhil tells him. Mudhil's sullen representations of the Arabs obtrude over and over throughout the novel. At the very end of the book he assures himself, in much the same way as he assures Ishmael, that "Hate is our [i.e., the Arabs'] overpowering legacy and we have regenerated ourselves by hatred .... In ten, twenty, thirty years the world of Islam will begin to consume itself in madness. We cannot live with ourselves .... we never have" (p. 564). The final verdict, as Haj Ibrahim puts it, is: "Hatred is holy in this part of the world. It is also eternal" (p. 60), and the Haj reverts at the end to a brutal custom of performing a ritual murder that eventually leads to a most fatal catastrophe embracing himself.

In the domain of the mass media and popular culture, the idea of a Muslim Orient has also left a mark no less indelible, and another unflattering picture, economic and political in nature, has been born out of the stereotypical images that the American imagination had for years entertained of the exotic Muslim East. The media now and then tend to perpetuate representations of the Arabs as incredibly wealthy, as barbaric and uncivilized; as sex maniacs; as blood-thirsty terrorists. To be an Arab is to be occasionally ridiculed in motion pictures, cartoons, magazines, and popular novels. Mostly, stereotypical images consist of veiled harems, cowards, non-progressive Bedouins, oil wells, camels, and white gowns. Undoubtedly, such pictures provide not only distorted information of one kind or another, but they also reinforce and sharpen the public's ideas of "the Muslim," "the Arab," "the Turk," "the Persian," and "the Near-Eastern" in general.[4]

For many centuries, however, the Muslim Orient has in effect constituted for the West an exotic, and often fabulous, entity, an alien, if somewhat confrontational, alternative World. The impact of the idea of a Muslim East on the Christian West can be traced back to the most climactic confrontation in the Middle Ages--the Crusades (1095-1291). But we learn from current conflicts in the region (the Crisis in the Gulf, the on-going Civil War in Lebanon, the *Intifada* in the West Bank in Palestine, Hezbollah in South Lebanon, and the Hamas warfare) that wars based on religious beliefs are certainly capable of generating prolonged hostility, and hostility, in turn, generates further antipathy. In spite of recent developments, whether political or economical, in what is known about that strange other World, many Western attitudes of considerable antiquity have not yet lost their influence. Events such as the series of Arab-Israeli, and other related, conflicts have also given the West a renewed share of anxiety and concern. But rather than providing better opportunities for mutual tolerance (if not trust), contemporary East-West relations have, in some ways, followed certain religious, cultural, and historical ideas that have engendered further mistrust. However, the change of opinion in these ideas from the Middle Ages to the present time, has been very small: the new situation has encountered the traditional conflicts of ideas between the two worlds, and thus the centuries-old attitudes led to a widespread misunderstanding of this diverse and complex group of nations and peoples and simultaneously to a coetaneous reluctance to change the situation.

It is within this confused and confusing context that the Muslim Orient and American culture confront each other. That there should be misunderstanding and anxiety on both sides is hardly surprising, as reflecting the general situation. This feeling has been further strengthened by the so called "Ethnic Cleansing" perpetrated by the Bosnian Serbs on the Muslims in former Yugoslavia with the connivance and a policy of "Masterly Inactivity" of the Christian West. No less astounding is what is recently happening in Chechenya and other Muslim republics of the former Soviet Union. But that is another story, and much of the significance of the study of the American reception, and misrepresentation of, the Muslim Orient remains, in and of itself, an attempt at a better understanding of the Muslim East -- it is hoped.

Notes

1 *Lydia Bailey* (New York: Doubleday and Co., 1947), pp. 313-314. Hereafter page numbers from this edition are in the text.

2 *The Nile* (New York: Simon and Schuster, 1983). Other quotations in the text follow this edition.

3 *The Haj* (New York: Doubleday and Co., 1984), pp. 545-546. See also pp. 49, 60, 108, 136, 466.

4 See, for a stimulating study, Jack G. Shaheen's *The TV Arab* (Ohio: Bowling Green State University Press, 1984), and, for a more in-depth, careful analysis, Edward W. Said's *Covering Islam: How the Media and the Experts Determine How We See the Rest of the World* (New York: Pantheon Books 1981).

BIBLIOGRAPHY

PRIMARY SOURCES

American

Alger, William R. *The Poetry of the East*. Boston: Whittemore, Niles, and Hall, 1856.

Baum, Maud Gage. *In Other Lands Than Ours*. Chicago, 1907. Reprint. New York: Scholars' Facsimiles and Reprints, 1983.

Brougham, John. *A Basket of Chips*. New York: Bunce and Brother, 1855.

Browne, John Ross. *Yusef; or, The Journey of the Frangi: A Crusade in the East*. New York: Harper and Brothers, 1853.

Bryant, William Cullern. *Letters from the East*. New York: G. Putnam and Son, 1869;

    ed. *Tales of Glauber-Spa: By Several American Authors*. The American Short Story Series, no. 38, 1832. Reprint. New York: Mass. Information Corporation, 1964.

Bulliet, Richard W. *Kicked to Death by a Camel*. New York: Harper and Row, 1973.

    The Tomb of the Twelfth Imam. New York: Harper and Row, 1979.

Burton, Richard Francis. *Personal Narrative of a Pilgrimage to al-Madinah and Meccah*. (1854) Tylston & Edwards, 1893. Reprint. New York: Dover Publications, 1964.

Clemens, Samuel L. *The Innocents Abroad; or, the New Pilgrim's Progress*. Vols. 1 and 2, *The Wirings of Mark Twain*. New York: Harper and Brothers, 1917.

Cobb, Sylvanus. *Ben Hamed; or, Children of Fate*. Boston: Elliot, Thomas and Talbot, 1863.

Cox, Samule S. *Orient Sunbeams*. New York: G.P. Putnam's Sons, 1882.

Curtis, George William. *The Howadji in Syria*. New York: Harper and Brothers, 1877.

Nile Notes of a Howadji. New York: Harper and Brothers, 1856.

De Forest, John W. *Irene, the Missionary.* Boston: Roberts Brothers, 1879.

Oriental Acquaintance; or, Letters from Syria. New York: Dix, Edwards and Co., 1856.

Digges, Thomas Atwood. *Adventures of Alonso...By a Native of Maryland....* 2 Vols. London, 1775, Reprint. New York: U.S. Catholic Historical Soceity, 1943.

Devine, Laurie. *The Nile.* New York: Simon and Schuster, 1983.

Dos Passos, John. *Orient Express.* New York: Cape and Smith, 1930.

Emerson, Ralph Waldo. *The Collected Works of Ralph Waldo Emerson.* Vols. 1-3. Edited by Alfred R. Ferguson. Cambridge: Belknap Press of Harvard Univ. 1971.

The Complete Works of Ralph Waldo Emerson [Centenary Edition]. 12 vols. Edited by Edward W. Emerson. Boston: Houghton Mifflin, 1903-1904.

The Correspondence of Emerson and Carlyle. Edited by Joseph Slater. New York: Columbia Univ. Press, 1964.

The Journals and Miscellaneous Notebooks of Ralph Waldo Emerson. 16 vols. Edited by William H. Gilman et al. Cambridge: Belknap Press of Harvard Univ., 1960-1982.

The Letters of Ralph Waldo Emerison. 6 vols. Edited by Ralph L. Rusk. New York: Columbia Univ. Press, 1939.

The Uncollected Lectures by Ralph Waldo Emerson. Edited by Clarence Gohdes. New York: William E. Rudge, 1932.

Forbes, Rosita. *The Sultan of the Mountains: The Life Story of Raisuli.* New York: Henry Hold and Co., 1924.

Franklin, Benjamin. "An Arabian Tale." In *The Works of Benjamin Franklin*, edited by John Bigelow, vol. 7, 387-88. New York: G.P. Putnam's Sons, 1904.

"A Narrative of the Late Massacres.... " In *The Works of Benjamin Franklin*, edited by John Bigelow, vol. 4, 22-48.

"On the Slave Trade." In *The Works of Benjamin Franklin*, edited by John Bigelow, vol. 12, 187-92. New York: G.P. Putnam's Sons, 1904.

Goodell, William. *Forty Years in the Turkish Empire; or, Memories of Rev. William Goodell.* Edited by E.G. Prime. New York: Robert Carter and Brothers, 1876.

Hooker, Edward W. *Memoir of Mrs. Sarah L. Huntington Smith, Late of the American Mission in Syria*, 3rd ed. New York: American Tract Society, 1845.

Howe, William W. *The Pasha Papers*. New York: Charles Scribner, 1859.

Humanity in Algiers; or, The Story of Azem. [By an American, Late a Slave in Algiers.] Troy: R. Moffitt and Co., 1801.

Irving, Washington. *Abu Hassan*. First published in 1924. In *Miscellaneous Writings 1803-1859*, edited by Wayne R. Kime, vol. 1, 192-277. Boston: Twayne Publishers, 1981.

A Chronicle of the Conquest of Granada. 1829. In *The Works of Washington Irving*, vol. 3, New York: P.F. Collier and Son, n.d.

Letters. 4 vols. Edited by Ralph M. Aderman, Boston: Twayne Publishes, 1978-1982.

Mahomet and His Sucessors. 1849-1850. 2 vols. Edited by Henry A. Pochmann and E.N. Feltskog. Madison: Univ. of Wisconsin Press, 1970.

Irving, Washington et al. *Salmagundi*. 1807. Edited by Bruce I. Granger and Martha Hartzog. Boston: Twayne Publishes, 1977.

Jessup, Henry H. *The Women of the Arabs*. New York: Dodd and Mead Publishes, 1873.

Jones, Joseph S. *The Usurpers; or, Americans in Tripoli*. 1835. In *America's Lost Plays*, vol. 14, 143-74. Bloomington: Indiana Unvi. Press, 1965.

Lowell, Hames Russell. *The Poetical Works of James Russell Lowell*. 5 vols. Cambridge: The Riverside Press, 1904.

Mailer, Norman, *Barbary Shore*. New York: Rinehart and Co., 1951.

Mayo, William Starbuck. *The Berber; or, The mountaineer of the Atlas: A Tale of Morocco*. New York: G.P. Putnam, 1850.

McFee, William. *North of Suez*. New York: Doubleday, Doran and Co., 1930.

Melville, Herman. *Clarel: a Poem and Pilgrimage in the Holy Land*. 1876. Edited by Walter E. Bezanson. New York: Hendricks House, 1960.

Miles, George H. *Mohammed, The Arabian Prophet: A Tragedy in Five Acts*. Boston: Philips and Co., 1850.

Miller, Joaquin. *Songs of the Sunlands*. Boston: Roberts Brothers, 1873.

Paulding, James Kirke. *Selim, The Benefactor of Mankind*. In *Tales of Glauber-Spa*, edited by William Cullen Bryant. New York: J. and J. Harper, 1832. Reprint, ii, 155-220. New York: Garret Press, 1969.

Payne, John Howard. *The Fall of Algiers*. London: John Cumberland, 182-.

Prime, William C. *Boat Life in Egypt and Nubia*. New York: Harper and Brothers, 1868.

Ray, William. *Poems, to Which is Added a Brief Sketch of the Author's Life, and of His Captivity and sufferings Among the Turks and Barbarians of Tripoli, on the Coast of Africa*. Arburn: U.F. Doubleday, 1821.

Reid, Mayne. *The Boy Slaves*. New York: Thomas R. Knox and Co., 1885.

Roberts, Kenneth. *Lydia Bailey*. New York: Doubleday and Co., 1947.

Smith, Richard P. *The Bombardment of Algiers*. 1829. In *America's Lost Plays*, vol. 13, 31-83. Bloomington: Indiana Univ. Press, 1965.

Stephens, John L. *Incidents of Travel in Egypt, Arabia Petraea and the Holy Land*. 8th ed. 2 vols. New York: Harper and Brothrs, 1867.

   Incidents of Travel in Greece, Turkey, Russia and Poland. 2nd ed. 2 vols. New York: Harper and Brothers, 1838.

Stoddard, Charles Warren. *A Cruise under the Crescent: From Suez to San Marco*. Chicago: Rand, McNally, 1898.

   Mashallah!: A Flight into Egypt. New York: D. Appleton, 1881.

Stoddard, Richard Henry. *The Book of the East*. In *The Poems of Richard Henry Stoddard*. New York: Charles Scribner's Sons, 1882.

Taylor, Bayard. *Central Africa*. New York: Putnam and Sons, 1875.

   Egypt and Iceland. New York: Putnam's Sons 1879.

   Lands of the Saracen. New York: Putnam's 1882.

   Poems of the Orient. Boston: Ticknor and Fields, 1855.

Tyler, Royall. *The Algerine Captive*. 1797. Edited by Don L. Cook. New Haven, Conn.: College and University Press, 1970.

Uris, Leon. *The Haj*. New York: Doubleday and Co., 1984.

Wallace, Lew. *The Prince of India*. 2 vols. New York: Harper and Brothers, 1893.

Ware, William. *Zenobia; or, the Fall of Palmyra*. 2 vols. New York: Francis and Co., 1850.

Warner, Charles Dudley. *In the Levant*. Vol. 4, *The Complete Writings of Charles Dudley Warner*. Harford, Conn.: The American Publishing Co., 1904.

   My Winter on the Nile. Vol. 3, *The Complete Writings*. Hartford, Conn.: The American Publishing Co., 1904.

Warton, Edith. *In Morocco*. New York: Charles Scribner's Sons, 1920.

Whittier, John Greenleaf. *The Poetical Works of Whittier*. Edited by Hyatt M. Waggoner. Boston: Houghton Mifflin, 1975.

Willis, Nathaniel P. *Pencillings by the Way*. 2 vols. Philadelphia: Carey, Lea, and Blanchard, 1836.

Winspear, Violet. *The Sheik's Captive*. New York: Harlequin Books, 1979.

European

Bacon, Francis. *The Works of Francis Bacon*. 10 vols. London: H. Bryer, 1803.

Beckford, William. *Vathek*. 1786. Edited by Roger Lonsdale. London: Oxford University Press, 1970.

Byron, George Gordon. *The Complete Poetical Works*. 3 vols. Edited by Jerome J. McGann. London: Oxford University Press, 1980.

The Works of Lord Byron: Letters and Journals. 6 vols. Edited by Rowland E. Prothero. London: J. Murray, 1898-1901.

Carlyle, Thomas. *Heroes, Hero-Worship, and the Heroic in History*. 1897. Rep. New York: AMS Press, 1974.

Dante, Alighieri. *The Inferno of Dante*. Trans. by Lacy Lockert. Princeton: Princeton Univ. Press. 1959.

Dryden, John. *The Conqeust of Granada by the Spaniards*. 1670-1671. In *John Dryden: Three Plays*, edited by George Saintsbury. New York: Hill and Wang, 1957.

Don Sebastian. 1690. In *Four Tragedies*, edited by L.A. Beaurline and Fredson Bowers. Chicago: Univ. of Chicago Press, 1967.

Kinglake Alexander Williams. *Eothen; or, Traces of Travel Brought from the East*. New York: Putnam, 1850.

Lane, Edward W. *An Account of the Manners and Customs of the Modern Egyptians*. London, 1837.

Lawrence, T.E. *Seven Pillars of Wisdom: A Triumph*. London: Jonathan Cape, 1935.

Lydgate, John. *Fall of Princes*. 4 vols. Edited by Henry Bergen. London: EETSES 1924-1927.

Marlowe, Christopher. *Tamburlaine the Great*. 1590. Edited by J.S. Cunningham. Manchester: Manchester Univ. Press, 1981.

Moore, Thomas. *Lalla Rookh.* London: Longman, Hurst, and Brown, 1817.

Poem of the Cid. Trans. by Rita Hamilton and Janet Perry. Manchester: Manchester Univ. Press, 1975.

The Song of Roland. Trans. by D.D.R. Owen. The Oxford Text, London: George Allen and Unwin Ltd., 1972.

Southey, Robert. *Poetical Works.* 10 vols. London: Longman, Orme, Brown, Green, and Longmans, 1838.

  Selections from the Letters of Robert Southey. 4 vols. Edited by John Wood Warter. London: Longman, Brown, Green, and Longmans, 1856.

Voltaire, Francois Marie Arouet. *Mahomet the Prophet; or, Fanaticism.* 1742. Trans. by Robert L. Myers. New York: F. Ungar Publishing Co., 1964.

Secondary Sources

Addison, James T. *The Christian Approach to the Moslem.* New York: Columbia Univ. Press, 1942.

Al-Aqiqi, Najib. *[The Orientalists...]* (in Arabic). 3rd ed. 3 vols. Cairo: Dar al-Ma'arif, 1965.

Al-Farsy, Layla Abdel al-Salam. "Washington Irving's *Mahomet*: A Study of the Sources." Ph.D. diss., University of Wisconsin, Milwaukee, 1983.

Andrae, Tor. *Mohammed: The man and His Faith.* Trans. by Theophil Menzel. London: George Allen and Unwin Ltd, 1936.

Attebery, A.J. *Oriental Essays: Portraits of Seven Scholars.* New York: Macmillan Co., 1960.

Attebery, Brian. *The Fantasy Tradition in American Literature: From Irving to Le Guin.* Bloomington: Indiana Univ. Prerss, 1980.

Baldwin, Marshall W. "Western Attitudes toward Islam." *The Catholic Historical Review* 27 (1942): 403-11.

Barnby, Henry G. *The Prisoners of Algiers: An Account of the Forgotten American-Algerian War,* 1785-97. London: Oxford Univ. Press, 1966.

Barrows, John H., ed. *The World's Parliament of Religions ....* 2 vols. Chicago: Parliament Publishing Co., 1893.

Barton, George A. *The Religions of the World.* 3rd ed. Chicago: Univ. of Chicago Press, 1929.

Barton, James L. *The Christian Approach to Islam.* Boston: Pilgrim Press, 1918.

Becker, C.H. and H.J. Chaytor. *Christianity and Islam.* New York: B. Franklin Press, 1974.

Blake, Patricia. "Lured by the Exotic East." *Time,* 3 September 1984, 84-85.

Brown, Wallae Cable. "The Popularity of English Travel Books About the Near East 1775-1825." *Philological Quarterly* 15 (1936): 70-80.

Burns, Robert I. "Christian-Islamic Confrontation in the West." *American Historical Review* 76 (June-December 1971): 1386-1434.

Cambridge History of Islam. 4 vols. London: Cambridge Univ. Press, 1970.

Carpenter, Frederick I. *Emerson and Asia.* Cambridge: Harvard Univ. Press, 1930.

Cash, William W. *Christendom and Islam.* New York: Harper, 1937.

Charvat, William. *The Origins of American Critical Thought, 1810-1835.* Philadelphia: Univ. of Pennsylvania Press, 1935.

Chejne, Anwar G. *Islam and the West, the Moriscos: A Cultural and Social History.* Albany: State Univ. of New York Press, 1983.

Muslim Spain. Minneapolis: Univ. of Minnesota Press, 1974.

Chew, Samuel C. *The Crescent and the Rose: Islam in England during the Renaissance.* New York: Oxford Univ. Press, 1937.

Child, Lydia M. *The Progress of Religious Ideas through the Successive Ages.* 3 vols. New York: C.S. Francis, 1855.

Christison, Kathleen. "The Arab in Recent Popular Fiction." *The Middle East Journal* 41, no. 3 (1987): 397-411.

Christy, Arthur. "Emerson's Debt to the Orient." *The Monist* 38 (January 1928): 38-64.

"Orientalism in New England: Whittier." *American Literature* (1929-30): 372-92.

"The Orientalism of Whittier." *American Litrature* 5 (1933-34): 247-57.

The Orient in American Transcendentalism: A Study of Emerson, Thoreau and Alcott. New York: Columbia Univ. Press, 1932.

Christy, Arthur, ed. *The Asian Legacy and American Life.* New York: John Day, 1942.

141

Clarice, James F. *Ten Great Religions: An Essay in Comparative Theology.* Boston: James R. Osgood, 1871.

Coles, Paul. *The Ottoman Impact on Europe.* New York: Harcourt, Brace, and World, 1968.

Conant, Martha P. *The Oriental Tale in England in the Eighteenth Century.* New York: Columbia Univ. Press, 1908.

Conway, Moncure D. *My Pilgrimage to the Wise Men of the East.* Boston: Houghton Mifflin, 1906.

Cook, Michael. *Muhammad.* London: Oxford Univ. Press, 1983.

Cox, Harvey. "Understanding Islam." *The Atlantic,* January 1981, 73-80.

Cutler, Allan. "The First Crusade and the Idea of Conversion." *Muslim Word* 58 (1968): 57-71.

Daniel, Norman, *Islam and the West: the Making of an Image.* Edinburgh: Edinburgh Univ. Press, 1960.

"Learned and Popular Attitudes to the Arabs in the Middle Ages." *Journal of the Royal Asiatic Society* (1977): 41-52.

Deledalle-Rhodes, J. "The Image of Islam in Nineteenth-Century Travel Literature." *International Journal of Moral and Social Studies* 1 (1986): 265-80.

Disuqi, Rasha. "Orientalism in Moby Dick." *American Journal of Islamic Social Sciences* 4, no. 1 (1987): 117-25.

Edwards, Michael, ed. T*he Life of Muhammad.* London: Folio Society, 1964.

Encyclopedia of Islam. 4 vols. Leyden: E.J. Brill, 1913-36.

Field, James A. *America and the Mediterranean World, 1776-1882.* Princeton: Princeton Univ. Press, 1969.

Finkelstein, Dorothee Metlitsky. *The Matter of Araby in Medieval England.* New Haven: Yale Univ. Press, 1977.

Melville's Orienda. New Haven: Yale Univ. Press, 1961.

Finnie, David H. *Pioneers East: The Early American Experience in the Middle East.* Cambridge: Harvard Univ. Press, 1967.

Fisher, Sir Godfrey. *Barbary Legend: War, Trade and Piracy in North Africa, 1415-1830.* Oxford: Clarendon Press, 1957.

Fleck, Richard F. "The Complexities of Mark Twain's Near Eastern Stereotyping". *Mark Twain Journal* 21 (1982): 13-15.

Friedman, Ellen G. *Spanish Captives in North Africa In the Early Modern Age.* Madison: Univ. of Wisconsin Press, 1983.

Ganzel, Dewey. *Mark Twain Abroad.* Chicago: Univ. of Chicago Press, 1968.

Gibb, H.A.R. *Mohammedanism.* 2nd ed. New York: Oxford Univ. Press, 1962.

Studies on the Civilization of Islam: Boston: Beacon Press, 1962.

Gibbon, Edward. *Life of Mahomet.* New York: Houghton Mifflin, n.d.

Gilmore, Myron P. *The World of Humanism,* 1453-1517. New York: Harper and Row, 1952.

Greenfield, Meg. "Our Ugly Arab Complex." *Newsweek,* December 5, 1977, 110.

Haykal, Muhammad H. *The Life of Muhammad.* Trans. by Ismail al-Faruqi. North American Trust Publications, 1976.

Hellal, Farida. "Emerson's Knowledge and Use of Islamic Literature." Ph.D. diss., University of Houston, 1971.

Herric, George F. *Christian and Mohammedan.* New York: Revell Co., 1912.

Hitti, Philip. *Islam and the West.* Princeton Univ. Press, 1962.

Hollenbach, John. "The Image of the Arab in Nineteenth-Century English and Americn Literature." *The Muslim World* 62 (1972): 195-208.

Hurgronje, C. Snouck. *Mohammedanism.* New York: G.P. Putnam's Sons, 1916.

Hussain, Asaf and Robert Olson, eds. *Orientalism, Islam, and Islamists.* Brattleboro, Vt.: Amana Books, 1984.

Isnai, Mukhtar Ali. "Cotton Mather and the Orient." *New England Quarterly* 43 (March-December 1970): 46-58.

"The Oriental Tale in American through 1865: A Study in American Fiction." Ph.D. diss., Princeton University, 1962.

Jackson, Carl T. "The Influene of Asia upon American Thought: a Bibliographcal Essay." *American Studies International* 22, no. 1 (April 1984): 3-31.

The Oriental Religions and American Thought: Nineteenth-Century Explorations. Estport, Conn.: Greenwood Press, 1981.

Jones, Meredith. "The Conventional Saracen of the Song of Geste." *Speculum* 17 (1942): 201-25.

Kabbani, Rana. "Eastern Travelogues: The Cultural Foundation of Colonialism." *Arab Affairs* 1, no. 1 (1986): 37-45.

Europe's Myths of Orient. Divide and Rule. London: Macmillan, 1986.

Kagle, Steven E. *America: Exploration and Travel.* Bowling Green: Bowling Green State Univ. Press, 1979.

Kateregga, Badru D. and David W. Shenk. *Islam and Christianity: A Muslim and a Christian in Dialogue.* Michigan: William B. Eardmans Publishing Co., 1981.

Kedar, Benjamin Z. *Crusade and Mission: European Appraoches Toward the Muslims.* Princeton: Princeton Univ. Press, 1984.

Lasater, Alice E. *Spain to England.* Jackson: Univ. Press of Mississippi, 1974.

Lewis, Bernard. *The Middle East and the West.* Bloomington: Indiana Univ. Press, 1964.

Lings, Martin. *Muhammad: His Life Based on the Earliest Soruces.* New York: Inner Traditions International 1983.

Lord, John. "Mohammad: Saracenic Conquests." In *Beacon Lights of History,* vol. 2, 23-54. New York: Fords, Howard, and Hulbert, 1885.

McClary, Ben H., ed. *Washington Irving and the House of Murry.* Knoxville: Univ. of Tennessee Press, 1969.

Meester, Marie E. *Oriental Influences in the English Literature of the Nineteenth Century.* Heidelberg, 1915.

Mortimer, Edward. "Islam and the Western Journalist." *The Middle East Journal* 35 (Autumn 1981): 492-505.

Mueller, Roger C. "The Orient in American Transcendental Periodicals." Ph.D. diss., University of Minnesota, 1968.

Muir, William. *Mahomet and Islam.* London: Longman, 1976.

Obeidat, Marwan M. "Arabic and the West. " To appear in the July-October 1996 issue of *The Muslim World.*

"The Image of Islam in Whittier's Poetry." *International Journal of Islamic and Arabic Studies* 1, no. 2 (1984): 31-40.

"In Search of the Orient: The Muslim East on the Contemporary American Literary Scene." *International Journal of Islamic and Arabic Studies* 3, no. (1986): 43-49.

"John Ross Brown: An Example of Nineteenth-Century American Residential Orientalism" (in Arabic). *al-Fikr al-Arabi,* June 1988.

"Lured by the Exotic Levant: The Muslim East to the American Traveler of the Nineteenth Century." *Islamic Quarterly* 31, no. 3 (1987): 168-193.

"Ralph Waldo Emerson and the Muslim Orient." *Muslim World* no. 2 (1988): 132-145.

"A Reflection on and Analysis of Western Literary Sources on Islam." *International Journal of Islamic and Arabic Studies* 2, no. 2 (1985): 47-67.

"Royall Tyler's *The Algerine Captive:* An Example of America's Early Literary Awareness of the Muslim Near East." *The American Journal of Islamic Social Sciences* 5, no. 1 (1988).

"Washington Irving and Muslim Spain." *International Journal of Islamic and Arabic Studies* 4, no. 1 (1987): 27-44.

Ockley, Simon. *History of the Saracens.* 2 vols. 1718. Reprint. London: G. Bell and Sons, 1878.

"Orientalism: The History, the Approach, and the Image" (in Arabic). *Al-Fikr al-Arabi* 32 (April-June 1983).

Orfalea, Gregory. "Literary Devolution: The Arab in Post-World War II Novel in English." *Journal of Palestine Studies* 17, no. 2 (1988): 109-28.

Oxtoby, Willard G. "Western Perceptions of Islam and the Arabs." In *The American Media and the Arabs,* Edited by Michael C. Hudson and Ronald G. Wolfe. Washington, D.C.: Georgetown University, 1980.

Pawley, D. "Never the Twain." *ARAMCO World Magazine* 37, no. 3 (1986): 28-33.

Pearce, Roy Harvey. "The Significance of the Captivity Narrative." *American Literature* 19 (1947): 1-20.

Playfair, R. Lambert. *The Scourge of Christendom.* London: Smith, Elder & Co., 1984.

Prideaux, Himphrey. *The True Nature of Imposture.* London: E. Curll, 1723.

Rejeb, Lofti Ben. " 'To the Shros of Tripoli' : The Impact of Barbary on Early American Nationalism." Ph.D. diss., Indiana University, 1981.

Riley-Smith, Jonathan. *What Were the Crusades?* London: Macmillan, 1977.

Rusk, Ralph L. *The Life of Ralph Waldo Emerson.* New York: Charles Scribner's Sons, 1949.

Said, Edward. *Covering Islam: How the Media and the Experts Determine How We See the Rest of the World.* New York: Pantheon Books, 1981.

Culture and Imperialism. London: Vintage Books, 1994.

Orientalism. New York: Vintage Books, 1979.

"The Phoney Islamic Threat." *New York Times Sunday Magazine*. November 21, 1993.

Sale, George, trans. *The Koran: Commonly Called the Alcoran of Mohammed... to Which is Prefixed a Preliminary Discourse*. 6th ed. Philadelphia: Lippincott, 1876.

Schacht, Joseph, ed. *The Legacy of Islam*. 2nd ed. London: Oxford Univ. Press, 1974.

Schoebel, Robert. *The Shadow of the Crescent: The Renaissance Image of the Turk*. Nien W. Koop, 1967.

Semann, Khalil I., ed. *Islam and the Medieval West: Aspects of Intercultural Relations*. Albany: State Univ. of New York Press, 1980.

Sha'ban, Fuad. *Islam and Arabs in Early American Thought: the Roots of Orientalism in America*. Durham, North Carolina: The Acron Press, 1991.

Shaheen, Jack G. *The TV Arab*. Bowling Green: Bowling Green State Univ. Press, 1984.

Sinor, Denis, ed. *Orientalism and History*. 2nd ed. Bloomington: Indiana Univ. Press, 1970.

Slade, Shelley, "The Image of the Arab in America." *The Middle East Journal* 35 (Spring 1981): 143-62.

Smith, Byron Porter. *Islam in English Literature*. Beirut: American Press, 1939.

Smith, Reginald Bosworth. *Mohammed and Mohammedanism*. 3rd ed. London: John Murray, 1889.

Smith, Wilfred Cartwell, *Islam in Modern History*. Princeton: Princeton Univ. Press, 1957.

Southern, R.W. *Western Views of Islam in the Middle Ages*. Cambridge: Harvard Univ. Press, 1962.

Spiller, Robert E. et al., eds. *The Literary History of the United States*. 1946. Reprint. rev. 4th ed. New York: Macmillan Publishing Co., Inc., and London: Collier Macmillan Publishers, 1978.

Tatlock, J.S.P. "Mohammed and His Followers in Dante." *Modern Language Review* 27 (1932): 186-95.

Tibawi, A.L. *American Interests in Syria, 1800-1901*. London: Oxford Univ. Press, 1966.

Turner, Bryan S. "Accounting for the Orient." In *Islam in the Modern World*, edited by Denis MacEoin and Ahmed Al-Shahi. New York: St. Martin's Press, 1983.

Marx and the End of Orientalism. London: George Allen and Unwin, 1978.

Voorhis, John W. "The Discussion of a Christian and a Saracen." *Muslim World* 25 (July 1935): 266-73.

"John of Damascus on the Moslem Heresy." *Muslim World* 24 (October 1934): 391-398.

Walker, Franklin. *Irreverent Pilgrims: Melville, Browne, and Mark Twain in the Holy Land.* Seattle: Univ. of Washington Press, 1974.

Wan, Louis. "The Oriental in Elizabethan Drama." *Modern Philology* 12 (1915): 423-47.

Watson, Charles R. *What is This Moslem World?* New York: Friendship Press, 1937.

Watt, Montgomery. "Islam and the West." In *Islam in the Modern World,* edited by Denis MacEoin and Ahmed Al-Shahi. New York: St. Martin's Press, 1983.

"Muhammad in the Eyes of the West." *Boston University Journal* 22, no. 3 (1974): 61-67.

Williams, Stanley. *The Life of Washington Irving.* 2 vols. 1935. Reprint. New York: Octagon, 1971.

The Spanish Background of American Literature. 2 vols. New Haven: Yale Univ. Press, 1955.

Wolf, John B. *The Barbary Coast: Algiers Under the Turks, 1800-1830.* New York: W.W. Norton and Co., 1979.

Wright, Louis B., and Julia H. Macleod. *The First Americans in North Africa.* Princeton: Princeton Univ. Press, 1945.

Yohannan, J.D. "The Influence of Persian Poetry upon Emerson's Work." *American Literature* 15 (March 1943): 25-41.

Yu, Beongcheon. The *Great Circle: American Writers and the Orient.* Detroit: Wayne State Univ. Press, 1983.

Zwemer, Samuel M. *The Cross Above the Crescent: The Validity, Necessity, and Urgency of Missions to Moslems.* Michigan: Zondervan Publishing House, n.d.

Islam: A Challenge to Faith.... New York: Student Volunteer Movement, 1907.

Bei Fragen zur Produktsicherheit wenden Sie sich bitte an:
If you have any questions regarding product safety,
please contact:

Walter de Gruyter GmbH
Genthiner Straße 13
10785 Berlin
productsafety@degruyterbrill.com